By the Authors

From Those Wonderful Folks Who Gave You Pearl Harbor
An Italian Grows in Brooklyn

By Charles Sopkin

Money Talks
Seven Glorious Days, Seven Fun-Filled Nights
The Bank Book

An
ITALIAN
Grows in
BROOKLYN

An ITALIAN Grows in BROOKLYN

Jerry Della Femina
Charles Sopkin

Little, Brown and Company   *Boston—Toronto*

FIRST EDITION

T 11/78

LIBRARY OF CONGRESS CATALOGING IN PUBLICATION DATA

Della Femina, Jerry.
  An Italian grows in Brooklyn.

  1. Della Femina, Jerry. 2. Italian Americans—
New York (City)—Biography. 3. Italian Americans—
New York (City)—Social life and customs. 4. Brooklyn
—Biography. 5. Brooklyn—Social life and customs.
I. Sopkin, Charles, joint author. II. Title.
F129.B7D444   974.7'1'040924 [B]   78–11562
ISBN 0–316–17991–4

Designed by Janis Capone

Published simultaneously in Canada
by Little, Brown & Company (Canada) Limited

PRINTED IN THE UNITED STATES OF AMERICA

For Barbara and Victoria

An ITALIAN Grows in BROOKLYN

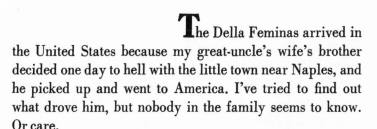

1

The Della Feminas arrived in the United States because my great-uncle's wife's brother decided one day to hell with the little town near Naples, and he picked up and went to America. I've tried to find out what drove him, but nobody in the family seems to know. Or care.

But once Gennaro Della Femina came to Mulberry Street in 1909, the migration started. He brought his sister over, and after the sister came his parents, and after the parents . . . Their village virtually emptied out. Cousins, aunts, uncles, brothers — the whole damn family picked up and, within a thirty-year span, came over. It has a lot to do with the Italian's inability to let anyone leave the family. They just pulled each other out of Italy. It wasn't that America's arms were outstretched, or that there were jobs. No, it was Gennaro's cousins, and my uncle, and my aunt's brother, and so they came; family was that strong with them. They could not survive in Italy without the family.

My family moved intact to the United States, but they kept their village habits and customs. They brought the old country with them, and in many ways it caused anguish. This anguish is sometimes known as the Italian Experience in the New World.

I have very mixed feelings about my "Italian Experience," and they are complicated enough for me to want to sit down and compare my experiences with those of the Irish, the Jews, the Germans, the Poles, and the other Europeans deposited by the massive waves of immigration to this country in the nineteenth century.

Several years ago, the Prince Spaghetti Company sponsored a charming but misleading commercial about a kid in Boston. In it, he is shown running home to lunch on Wednesday, so he can eat a piping hot bowl of Prince spaghetti, which, we are told, is absolutely tops with every Italian in the North End. ("Wednesday is Prince Spaghetti day." The heavy-handed implication is, if the pasta is good enough for the paisanos in Boston, why then it's good enough for you.) Even though it's midweek lunch, it looks like there are at least fifteen members of the family gathered around the table, which is okay, I suppose, for television, but it doesn't happen in real life.

I never came home for lunch on Wednesday, or any other day. Nobody did in the Gravesend section of Brooklyn. One Thursday I came home early, but that was because I'd been caught in a crap game in the hallway of Lafayette High School. A teacher had broken up the game and I literally ran all the way home to gather my wits. What I ended up doing was talking my mother out of a couple of dollars. I then ran to the barber shop where I got a crew cut, the purpose of which was to confuse my teacher, who would try to identify me as having participated in the crap game.

Our family only gathered for dinner — and I know that this was the same for all Italian families. Nobody got home for lunch, because everyone in the family was out trying to earn a living. And when we gathered for dinner, generally our faces weren't cheerful either. Dinner — any meal, actually — was for eating, and there was little idle gossip.

I think what bothered me, when I first saw that Prince commercial, was the almost complete absence of reality. I then began looking at other "Italian" commercials; and if I was offended by Prince, then that actor whose first name is Enzo singing the praises of Mama in a tomato sauce commercial was even more offensive.

Although I am an advertising man of Italian descent (as opposed to an Italian advertising man), I can't offer much of an explanation as to why the commercials advertising tomato sauce, spaghetti, and other Italian-oriented products are more cliché-ridden than any other. I realize that the American image of practically all ethnic groups is affected by fantasy; but the Italian image as perceived by others always has seemed the richest of all.

Fortunately for the Italian Tourist Bureau, Italy is blessed by a sunny climate and sunny dispositions from Positano to Parma. Yes, there is a Mafia over there — and over here — but for the most part they're right off the *Godfather II* set, except the Sicilian branch, and they're funny old men with shotguns.

The French are universally known for their cuisine,

their couture, their style, and their hostility, which knows no bounds. The Italians, on the other hand, seem to be grinning in every café throughout the country — at least if I am to believe the reports from tourists.

The Jews of America are less like Gertrude Berg than Irving Howe's immigrants. The Irish, German, and other immigrants perpetuate myths that have been accepted by the American culture. And the Italian myth is even more inaccurate, further from reality than the image created by any other immigration.

My father was born in this country — but just barely. His parents had been here for only a short while. My mother was brought here in 1915, when she was four years old. She settled on Mulberry Street in Manhattan, where a lot of the Neapolitans ended up. In her case, she was sponsored by the families who were involved with Angelo's Restaurant and Ferrara's Bakery & Confectionary. Mulberry and Mott Streets were literally halfway houses on the way to the Bronx, Queens, Staten Island, or Brooklyn, or Harlem, where there was a sizable contingent.

The Della Feminas ended up in the Gravesend section of Brooklyn, which was about a forty-square-block area ten minutes from Sheepshead Bay and Coney Island. It originally had been farmland, settled by the diligent and hardworking Dutch. The English followed. In the early twentieth century a family named Amici moved in, and the old settlers took one look at them — and *their* relatives — and eventually moved out.

It is engraved upon us that all of our forefathers came to this country because of the opportunity. We cannot shake the image of the crowds of people flooding through Ellis

Island, having their names casually changed by stern (but in some cases kind) customs officers who knew how to handle the rabble. All of us were leaving the land of the starving (Irish), the oppressed (Pilgrims, Jews, you name them). Everyone had come to the New World to seek his fortune, and if the streets weren't paved with gold, well, by God, then they were at least to be paved with asphalt from the Sicilian Asphalt Paving Company (a large New York firm).

The fact remains that every Italian friend of mine and absolutely all of my relatives were living a fairly substandard existence in Italy and they did not come to America to better themselves; rather, they arrived because of family ties.

We left because someone was here. One bachelor in a tiny village near Naples decided one day to pull up stakes and try America and within twenty years villages emptied out as effectively as if the plague had hit.

It is my contention that the Italians alone — of all the waves of immigration, including the most recent Puerto Rican influx — have never completely accepted the so-called American experience.

In 1911, the daughter did not leave home until she married. That has barely changed to this day. What happens in an astonishing number of families is that everyone is living in a two-story house and when the daughter gets married, she simply leaves to move upstairs, visiting the family on Saturday nights.

Practically every aspect of Italian life is depicted in one way (and not unfavorably, I might add), and yet the experience I had in growing up was exactly different.

I did not speak English until the age of six, and I don't

think I was the exception in my neighborhood. The family was the center of the universe and the neighborhood was the outer limits of the family. Some members of our family — to this day — have not been to the Bronx, parts of Queens. Manhattan is a mysterious, truly mysterious island.

Some years ago when I finally had a job that lasted more than three months, my wife and I decided to throw a party *for the family* — and all that it entailed. We invited everyone — and they all came to see how the Della Femina kid was managing in faraway Manhattan, doing something strange for a living, called advertising. There they were, sixty Brooklyn Italians, as desperately out of water as they could be. First of all, they'd never been to a cocktail party, and they didn't know what was expected of them. Second, they did not know from standing around and drinking. They all sat in the sixty gilt (or guilt!) chairs provided by the caterer, tried to eat the caterer's food (which was anathema to all of us), and then trekked back to Brooklyn, saying Jerry and Barbara seemed to be in a lot of trouble.

To this day, only a handful of guys from the neighborhood have made it out into a semblance of integrated society, including a sportswriter for the *Daily News* named Phil Pepe and me. Occasionally, Pepe and I meet each other and when we do, we have on occasion tried to decipher the Italian in America, as opposed to the Italian-American.

One of the starting places, at least in my experience, is in the treatment of the Mafia. My old neighborhood may well be the toughest neighborhood (white division) in the United States. In the 1950s, when the late Estes Kefauver was holding his celebrated hearings on crime in the United

States, he called Gravesend the "worst breeding ground for organized crime in the United States."

It might well have been that. What it truly was was the worst breeding ground for lower-middle-class nonentities in the United States, forget about the crime. However, organized crime and the Mafia are glamorous subjects and have a tendency to get all of the headlines. We had one hell of a lot of *violence* in the neighborhood, provoked and unprovoked. But in terms of the Mafia, it wasn't there.

I don't know what my parents whispered to each other late at night, but I doubt seriously whether it was that Angelo Missini had just become connected. We did not keep up with who was a button man and who wasn't in the Colombo Family.

We had crime, yes, gambling, oh God yes, murder, absolutely; but not much flashy talk about the Mafia. Those few members of the Mafia in our neighborhood lay very low and did their Mafiaing out of the neighborhood.

The real tragedy of the neighborhood was not crime but the crushing effect on ambition. For reasons not clear to me even today, the grinding poverty of Gravesend was, if anything, worse than that of Naples, or Palermo. It seemed to have a debilitating effect on people. And where other migrants seemed to move out and integrate into society, the Italians were slow about it, almost unmoving.

We are still menial laborers. Among us are far too few lawyers, doctors, engineers. It's as if some Higher Being looked at the United States and said, "Hey listen, the U.S. is short of cooks, waiters, shoe repairmen, and singers; let's put the Italians to work. And give me an order of fried zucchini to go." And that's what happened.

My own experience seems to have run counter to the

image time and time again. We were not — in our family, among friends and neighbors — so jolly and fun-filled. There aren't any singers in any of the outer reaches of my family. (We do have more than our share of unemployed, however.) If there ever was joy, there also was pain. Whenever any of us won a modest bet in gambling on the horses or playing the numbers, we always knew absolutely that a piece of bad luck would be coming our way the next day. Tit for tat.

Virginia Yans-McLaughlin, a professor of history at Sarah Lawrence, has spent some time studying the Italian immigrants to Buffalo, and she wrote a piece about her studies in the *New York Times*. Surprise! She discovered that the Italians were family-oriented:

But the historians' goal is not to replace one myth with another; they seek to correct a distorted historical image which views lower-class families as victims of poverty, unemployment and discrimination and to explain how people moving from traditional societies one generation ago ultimately assumed a conservative white working-class family culture. There is no need to romanticize or mystify this process. . . .

At least half of the Italian immigrant families who ultimately reunited in this country experienced five or six years of temporary separation; after arrival the families faced chronic unemployment, inadequate housing, low living standards, poor diets, high mortality rates and a constant struggle to support the six or seven children who did survive life's early years.

Yet the overwhelming majority of Italian families survived these difficulties without severe disorder. Compared to other groups, Italians produced fewer illegitimate births; they sought relief hesitantly, rarely citing desertion or nonsupport by the male bread winner as their justification. Desertion and divorce occurred rarely. . . . Finally, uprooting from south Italian villages did not diminish loyalty to kin; relatives helped one another to immigrate, they shared households, loaned money for business ventures and helped in job searches.

All of which is quite true. But what Dr. Yans-McLaughlin doesn't add is that a terrible price seemed to be paid for this apparent societal adjustment: lack of progress.

It is the Della Femina theory of southern Italian immigration (ca. 1875–1915) that the Italians actually brought their villages with them.

What no one has yet figured out is *why* we isolated ourselves; not one Italian I know has a logical explanation. If Dr. Yans-McLaughlin is just getting around to the fact that we were uprooted yet remained intact and loyal, I've got news for her: in our neighborhood we never felt we left the old country. When World War II came to our village, there was a real problem for most of my family — they weren't sure which side to root for.

This isolation, this "us against them" attitude, clings to me (at least a part of it) to this day. There is an Italian slang word — it sounds like *sfaccim'* — that means the sperm of the devil. My partner, Ron Travisano (who also is Italian), and I still use it to alert each other to some kind of hazard. For example, if someone approaches us and Ron wants to warn me about him, he will say very quietly, "*Sfaccim'*," and I'll know to be wary.

I truly believe that Italians rank right along with the black man as stereotypes: we also have rhythm, we sing (although we aren't noted for our dancing), we jive, we laugh, we have our language (although our hip language hasn't entered the mainstream of American slang the way black slang has) and we have a way with food.

As with all stereotypes, the Italian one is just as dangerous and devastating as is the Jewish or the black stereotype. All Jews aren't so astute with money, all blacks aren't so nimble on their feet, and there are one hell of a lot of Italian women out there who can't cook worth a damn.

Since we brought our village with us, we obeyed the law of the old land: never let the outsider know what you are doing or thinking. Just as feelings of hostility mingled with isolation exist today in many areas of southern Italy, the same feelings occur in Brooklyn.

I drive back to Avenue U and the old neighborhood just about every other week, and not long ago I brought a friend who had never been to that section of New York. My friend, whom I'll call Bob, was staggered at what he saw. From every doorway we were met with suspicious glances. The locals knew me — older guys who had grown up and left the neighborhood — but they sure didn't know Bob, and they checked him out very carefully.

We walked into a popular cigar store, at the back of which exist weekly high-stakes poker and crap games, and the moment we walked in all conversation came to a halt. As far as I'm concerned, we could have been in Italy. My friend and I walked past a so-called social club, also on Avenue U. The club is located in a storefront, and the two front windows have shades pulled halfway down. As we looked into the window, two deeply disturbed members of the club glared out at us and then pulled the shades all the way to the windowsill.

The faces could have been two kilometers from Palermo

and the look they gave us definitely was Sicilian in origin. In a word, they said, "Stay away."

I grew up in Gravesend not really understanding that there was a different world out there until I was eighteen. Because my father worked as a pressman for the *New York Times*, I was able to get a messenger's job in the newspaper's advertising department, and from that summer on, I decided that Manhattan was infinitely better than Gravesend and did everything in my power to achieve a life of my own in Manhattan.

I was fortunate. Today, many of the guys I grew up with are still back in Brooklyn, still hanging around the same cigar store, still shooting dice on Sundays, still betting on the horses.

It ought to be noted that there is some bitterness in the pages to follow. I wouldn't want readers to be misled into expecting an Italian version of *The Summer of '42*: warm, touching memories of a sensitive upbringing.

I once saw a man who had welshed to the bookies have his legs deliberately broken by two gorillas swinging tire chains — the beating taking place in full view of the neighborhood to serve as an object lesson to all of the would-be welshers of the community. This kind of casual violence tends to eliminate warm, fond memories rather quickly.

I have very strong views about the Church — and you can call it either the Church or the church, depending on your preference. My entire family walked away from the Church as rapidly as they could, and if you are deeply religious, or even deeply spiritual, perhaps you'd best skip chapter nine entirely.

Sex on the streets of Brooklyn tended — and tends — to be nonlyrical, nonpoetic, and sharply focused, rather than filmed through a gauzy filter. My views and my memories about the structured rituals of marriage, death, and other formal occasions tend, for the most part, to be accurate and not very sentimental.

We Italians *are* different from every other immigrant group, and although Dr. Yans-McLaughlin's book, which I haven't read, may have the whole thing figured out, it would surprise me.

I wish that I could say at the outset of this book that I've solved, once and for all, the enigma of the Italian. Obviously, I haven't. This is the experience of one Italian who slipped out from under; he left the neighborhood, the family, the society, the church.

People who have been baffled by the Italians are legion. One of the highlights (for me, anyway) of the Nixon transcripts was a plaintive Nixon expressing perpetual confusion about the worth of the Italian lira and crankily asking someone to explain the damned currency to him once and for all. And then there was that wonderful exchange when Nixon, desperately trying to figure out what to do with Judge Sirica, said plaintively to one of his aides, "He's Italian and I don't deal with them. They're not like us."

Indeed, Mr. Nixon, we are not.

2 ——————————————

My grandparents — all four of them — never did learn the language of their reluctantly adopted country. My grandmother did pull herself together and learn two words of English: "no home." It didn't matter who was at the door; "no home" was good enough for any busybody. She didn't learn English because she didn't think the country — or her coming over here — was going to work out. She kept thinking that it was temporary for the forty years she lived in America and remained thinking that until the day they buried her on foreign soil. She was sixty years old before she even *saw* the Borough of Queens and she went to her grave not knowing that the Bronx, Manhattan, or Staten Island existed.

Life revolved around family, the children, sickness, and death. There weren't any casual dinnertime discussions of politics because — and I say this categorically — not one of my grandparents ever knew who the President of the United States was, and this was during the four terms of Franklin D. Roosevelt. As for the conception of *why* they left Naples and came here, the word "freedom" didn't arise. All four grandparents came over here during the period from 1915 to 1918 and they lived contentedly as aliens until the Second World War, when all hell broke loose.

Suddenly, after twenty-five years in America, there was a war and their homeland was in it. My family had to go to the post office and register as aliens, but they didn't understand the procedure. There was tremendous turmoil in my house because no one in my family could understand the forms. And they had two months to fill them out; otherwise, they thought, back on the boat after twenty-five years of camping out in the United States.

The man who finally bailed them out was Charlie the Fruit Man. Charlie and his ancient truck came through the neighborhood every day with fresh produce, and he had more than a smattering of English because he had to deal with the markets to buy his produce. Nobody in the neighborhood went to the store to buy fruit and vegetables unless there was an emergency.

It was Charlie who helped them with the forms and who also patiently explained to everyone that the U.S. was at war, and that Italy was on the wrong side. There was a fantastic pro-Italian feeling in the neighborhood, and I, as a child, certainly did not know which side Italy was on. My grandmother always wore a large scarf that had Italy depicted on it as a woman who was embracing Germany, which was displayed as a man.

A guy named Luigi, who was the insurance man, also had a hand in the alien scare. Although the women were worried by the form, the men were paralyzed by it. And all they had to do was to get it over to the post office on Avenue U to turn the forms in. (Coincidentally, a group of unorganized neighborhood fascists met regularly upstairs in the post office and were never bothered, as far as I can find out. The same upstairs room of the post office became a reception room for weddings of the more modest sort.)

One day Luigi and Charlie got the forms in order, and both sets of my grandparents walked the one block to the post office as if it were the "last mile" in the Big House. They registered without too much trouble, because the entire post office staff spoke one dialect or another of Italian.

No sooner was the registration hurdle past than my uncle got drafted. My grandmother thought that once she got the forms turned in the whole thing would blow away; obviously, it didn't. Uncle Freddy got drafted in 1942, and it was the first time a member of my family got called in to serve in any army of any country.

Uncle Freddy's call to arms caused tremendous stress in the family. He lived in our house, along with my mother's parents, my brother, and myself. We were crowded but we had adequate space, and yet when Freddy was inducted in 1942 the house suddenly seemed empty. Neither my mother nor my grandmother understood what was going on, although they took comfort in the fact that Freddy was shipped to Alabama. Alabama was mysterious to my grandparents, although its saving grace was that the word itself ended in "a," as in marinara. But then Freddy was transferred to Fort Knox, Kentucky, and that was even more frightening. My grandmother couldn't pronounce Kentucky and, as far as she was concerned, Freddy was dead.

I was too young to try to explain that he really wasn't dead, he was just swallowed up by Kentucky. My mother wasn't so sure everything was going to be all right, either.

Despite my grandmother's unworldly ways, she ruled the house. She made most of the crucial family decisions. We all listened to her and everyone deferred to her. My grandfather spent his day drinking wine and smoking Di Nobile cigars, not contributing anything to the proceedings.

Like all Italian grandfathers throughout the world, he wore dark gray pants, a soiled white shirt, a sports jacket that did not match the pants, and black shoes. He never wore a sweater; that was for Jewish grandfathers.

Grandmother's expertise embraced when and what the family ate, what time they would go to sleep after eating whatever they ate, and bowel movements.

All of the grandmothers in the neighborhood would begin their day by brushing their teeth with salt. The old women were the first natural food advocates. Breakfast consisted of coffee and bread, the bread dipped into the coffee. The coffee was deep black. I did not learn about brown coffee until I was sixteen and happened to order a cup of coffee in a restaurant. When I added milk to the restaurant coffee, it turned brown. Up until then my notion of coffee was that it was a gray substance, the liquid originally being black but turning gray with the addition of milk.

We had eggs in the house, but they were never scrambled — always hard-boiled. We rarely used butter, and didn't keep it around. Among the other items you couldn't find in the house was ketchup. The consistency of ketchup was pretty close to that of the sauce you put on pasta, and who makes a cold sauce and then puts it into a bottle? The same thing for mayonnaise. It was disgusting to put something like that on tuna fish. By all rights you could die from such a combination.

Prince spaghetti was not featured at lunch. My mother might take an egg and combine it with yesterday's leftover macaroni to make a macaroni pie. Eggs were not used to make something foreign called an omelette. Eggs simply held other things together. Obviously, no one knew anything about cholesterol. It seemed to us that we had a pretty healthy diet. No one ever said, "Gee, we ought to have X amount of fiber in our diet." We gravitated toward fresh vegetables and fresh fruit. Nothing was ever thrown out; consequently there was no garbage, except for a few coffee grounds once a day.

When Charlie the Fruit Man came to your house and sold you fruit and vegetables, they weren't wastefully wrapped in acres of paper. You wanted Swiss chard, you got Swiss chard without any pretense. There were no prepackaged foods — they were against our religion. One summer night in 1947 my mother committed a sacrilege by bringing home a Betty Crocker apple pie mix. My grandmother, seeing Betty Crocker as a threat to both her sovereignty and her ability to run the house, started a tremendous fight. She predicted death and destruction if anyone ate the alien apple pie, and her prediction was made with the fervor of a gypsy.

My mother faced one of those watershed decisions. Should she go ahead and defy her mother and make the damn thing, or should she cave in and throw it out? So, with my grandmother absolutely enraged, my mother went ahead and cooked the pie and served it after dinner. My grandmother sat there predicting that the children would die. Whether it was voodoo or botulism, the entire family got deathly ill from the pie. It was the sickest I've ever been in my entire life. As I was throwing up that night, in between gasps for air I could hear my grandmother saying, "Don't cross me again. I can turn your milk into stone!" It was the last alien food to enter the house for a good ten years.

We didn't have any "snacks": Italians thought that a lot of fruit was the key to a safe and sane digestive tract. Many homes in the neighborhood had their own carefully tended fig trees, and our neighbors, the Calabreses, had a big backyard and planted an entire garden.

The family ate at 6:30 P.M on the dot. Grandmother sat at the head of the kitchen table and my parents were on either side of her. I sat at the foot of the table, and my grandfather sat to my right. He would knock down three or four glasses of wine and nod off right there at the table. We all drank a lot of red wine. A gallon would go *phtttt!* — like that. So we normally bought it by the five-gallon jug. White wine was thought to be very weak and thus the special wine of the Protestants. We were a total red-wine society and, believe me, there were no niceties about white wine with the chicken, etc. We had red wine with everything, and there were many who had red wine with nothing.

My first taste of wine was mixed with cream soda. We started drinking at a very early age. Children were regarded as old enough to drink when they were old enough to swallow. Italians everywhere — including Italy — place great faith in the restorative powers of wine. We feel that wine can perform great healing miracles in all areas of life: medical, sexual, cultural. You name it, wine fixes it. If our neighbor Bellitti had cancer, which he did, and couldn't eat, the neighborhood advice was, "Have a drink of wine." It was magic stuff, pure magic.

I can say without contradiction that our meals were without any redeeming social or educational value whatsoever. After all, most of us were trying to cope with macaroni and beans, plus greens and a meat dish. During the war, when meat was rationed, a staple at the table was fried sausage. On top of the war, we were poor, so my mother often bought beef heart. And if you get a bit queasy at the sound of heart, try something that graced many Italian tables called *cabutzel,* a terrific little dish made up of the head of a lamb.

It was the *cabutzel* that brought the grandfather to the center of the table. Until then, the grandmother ran things, doling out all the food from her position at the head of the table. But when the *cabutzel* hit the table, the younger generation started to groan and yell in protest; the lamb's head had been split right down the middle and then cooked. The family would be looking at the inside of the lamb's head (at least one half of it) and, while we were looking at the *cabutzel,* it was looking at us with its one cooked eye. The Arabs had nothing on the Italians when it came to barbaric eating practices. Just as everyone was about to faint at the sight of the half head with its dead eye, my trusty grandfather, laced out of his mind on a dozen jelly glasses of red wine, would pluck that eye out and eat the goddamn thing with a big flourish. We kids would scream, and my grandfather would then patiently explain that the eye was the delicacy.

My family wasn't the only one coping with lamb's eyes. I've talked with friends, and all of them remember having to fend with *cabutzel*. A recipe for *cabutzel* called for soaking the head (or half head) of the lamb for hours and hours in salt water — sometimes days if the demand for *cabutzel* wasn't particularly strong. After soaking, the thing was thrown into the oven and roasted. It was really quite good, although the taste loses something in description.

We always had a lot of fresh fish because the fishermen came through the neighborhood selling their catches. My family also was very big on razor clams, which come in a shell looking something like a straight razor. After they're opened, a couple of squirts of fresh lemon juice are dropped on them, and they move a bit. Not too much, because as soon as they start their move, I start mine and pop them into my mouth and bite hard. Very hard. (My wife was not raised on razor clams, and she wasn't prepared for their movement. When Barbara saw her first razor clam take a walk, she got hysterical and wouldn't kiss me for days.)

My grandfather was the neighborhood source for mussels. He had a pushcart and he sold fresh mussels every day. My other grandfather pushed vegetables. Bakery goods came through the street, as did the iceman, as did the butter-and-egg man who also carried Italian olive oil. If we sat on the front steps of our house long enough the entire meal would arrive. When we eventually produced a tiny amount of garbage, an Italian garbageman would be by eventually to take away what little we had.

There were no restaurants in our neighborhood: we

didn't go out to eat. We ate either at our house, or Cousin Ronnie's, or Uncle Dom's, or wherever. My grandmother would start making her meat sauce at seven in the morning on Sunday and within five or six hours that smell would be all through the house, covering everything — clothing, furniture, appliances — and then it would go out the front door and into the streets, to mix with the aroma of neighboring meat sauces. Except that, for some reason, we didn't call them "sauces"; we called them "gravies" rather than "sauces." I could enter the neighborhood at one end and sample the air quality of the gravy, and the odds were that it would be about the same at the other end of the neighborhood, with the exception of the Sicilians', who were strange in just about every other department, too. They were much more violent than the Neapolitans and as far as their dialect went, we couldn't understand a word they were saying. They ate weird things; at least we Neapolitans thought so. They ate macaroni with pumpkin, and who the hell would do something like that?

What little dinner table talk there was, was strictly Italian gossip. The entire conversation stayed within the confines of the neighborhood. There wasn't a recounting of the day's activities, because they were boring beyond belief. We did, though, discuss in detail the smallest piece of local news. "I hear Mrs. Caggiano is having a problem with her son," my mother once said. The entire family would then seize upon the Caggiano situation. Young Caggiano got caught breaking and entering and was about to "go away" for a while. That was a somber piece of news, and one that tended to depress the spirits of those at the table.

My grandmother could do a fast five minutes on the quality of the greens. "The greens were horrible today, I didn't get any," or, "The greens are as nice as they've been all year, eat!" While my grandparents were alive, there wasn't any sports talk at the table. After they died, the Yankees gradually came into the house.

My father worked as a pressman for the *New York Times* for forty years, and I don't think we ever had a copy in the house. He certainly didn't carry the trials and tribulations of his job home with him. But we really didn't need the *Times* for communication. Each street was a village, and since we were on West Seventh we needed to be filled in on what was going on on West Fifth Street and West Fourth. Although the streets looked alike, they did have their differences, and we needed to know what was going on in other quarters. My mother's first cousin, Mary, lived on West Third, and through her we were able to get some information from the outside.

Mary continually fought the "Establishment." She also made us laugh because when she went up against the Establishment she always managed to get a laugh (in Italian) at their expense. And who was the Establishment? Those people who spoke and understood English. Periodically, Mary also had battles with "the Jews," and when she made a reference like that we knew she was referring to a lawyer. All lawyers were Jewish to Mary, and she especially relished going up against them.

Although Mary seemed to have a tremendous gusto for life, she differed from just about the entire neighborhood in personality. My mother's mother was much more the norm in the neighborhood. Although I never heard my grandmother say, "I have a tough life," the expression on

her face was one of hostility. She was continually suspicious — of outside people, forces, and goods. As a kid
I would sit around and listen to my grandmother and her
cronies talk about dinner. They'd be sitting out on the
front sidewalk with huge pots next to them, cutting up
string beans. "I'm making string beans tonight," my grandmother would say. "Oh, you're making string beans,"
would come the reply, even though my grandmother was
sitting by a pile of string beans that you could see a block
away. "Yes, I'm making beans with lemon and oil." "Oh."
"I'm also making macaroni."

And so it went, the ladies sitting in a circle discussing
the food of the day. What I love about the neighborhood
and the old ladies who are still there to this day is that
there are terrific marketing guys at General Foods and
General Mills and Betty Crocker wondering why they can't
get their prefrozen, precooked, preshrunk, predigested stuff
into the old ladies' market baskets.

We didn't have frozen vegetables in the house until my
grandmother died at the age of eighty, and even then I'm
sure my mother went out to Queens to double check that
my grandmother was still in the grave before she started
bringing home Birds Eye. After all, my grandmother had
done such a job on us with the Betty Crocker cake mix
that none of us was eager to have another disaster on our
hands, and even I felt that a curse could be carried beyond the confines of the grave.

What staggers me about the grandmothers is that they
didn't complain too much about their lot in life. I've
finally come to the conclusion that the reason that they
didn't complain is that they really hadn't left Naples.

The location of the kettles had changed, but their life sure as hell hadn't. They talked about the old country, but no one — not a single person — ever seriously made a move to go back, because back there was *real* poverty, grinding no-end-in-sight poverty. But Brooklyn was still Italy as far as they were concerned. And the same went for us.

I don't know how my grandparents survived the trip from Italy. I do not know how they ever got past Ellis Island. Today, all of us do things that we take for granted, but in those days to fill out a form — like an application for a bank account — was agony. They left a country noted for its massive corruption of officials, and the people they ran into in this country weren't much better.

My grandparents didn't know how to buy anything on the installment plan, so they paid cash. They didn't use banks because they didn't trust banks. The Kings Highway Savings Bank in Brooklyn cleverly passed out account-application forms to the kids in school. All of the kids were instructed on how to fill the form out, and I thus became the first person in my family to have a bank account. Since Kings Highway Savings was in a Jewish neighborhood, my parents and grandparents were slightly uncomfortable going over there anyhow.

What savings my grandparents had were kept in the house, under the mattress. When someone in the neighborhood threw out a mattress, the garbagemen would find it slit open. Not that my family was worried about the banks closing. They weren't aware that they closed, or reopened, or that banks were stable. Utilities were covered by Brooklyn Union Gas & Electric — in cash. We had no telephone; the street's telephone was in Barney's candy store. They'd take the call for us and come running to the house to let us know the outside world was trying to get through.

We lived in a village cut off from the rest of the world, cut off as effectively as if we were hemmed in by an avalanche or an earthquake. But a perpetual earthquake. Somehow food arrived in our isolated village and neighbors helped each other out, as neighbors do in time of crisis. And in a crisis one of the most popular women in the neighborhood was my mother's second cousin, Mrs. Galento, who lived on West Fifth Street. She was one of the first in our family to lead the way from our village in Italy, and that gave her prestige among all of us. Her son, Anthony, was striving for something more. He wanted to be a lawyer, which, for that time and place, was a very heavy number. Anthony was a brilliant kid, but no one — *no one* — even thought about college, much less being a lawyer.

Mrs. Galento, in her own unsubtle way, told Anthony a thousand times to forget about being a lawyer. She also told him that if he kept reading, and if he kept studying, that vast amount of knowledge he was cramming into his head was going to make him insane.

My own mother, knowing of the struggle that was going on with Mrs. Galento and Cousin Anthony, would tell me not to read excessively, that it was bad for me. My mother and Mrs. Galento were terribly worried that Anthony was going to go insane with all of his studying. The Italian view of education went something like this: the mind was not a sponge (a figure of speech they rejected) but rather the brain was like a balloon. Thus, if you stuffed too much knowledge into that balloon, it was going to burst.

Anthony must have been pretty bright, because he got

good marks and finished high school. Because his family had a bit of money, he went on to a city college — and if finishing high school was a bit unusual, going to college was spectacular. At the end of his first year in college he flipped out. They came and took Cousin Anthony away, who sure enough had a real, full-blown nervous breakdown. During the tumult, his mother kept wailing, "Why did he have to study?" Her dramatic comment on the acquisition of knowledge was no doubt repeated many times in the years to come by grandmothers with grandchildren who showed a little too much desire to study.

Anthony had broken the code; he had tried to pursue a career and that just wasn't done. I can remember for months afterward his mother's coming over to our house and crying that his teachers hated him because he was a Catholic. When you put all the pieces together, it wasn't surprising that he cracked up; the only thing that amazed me was that he had been able to finish eight months of college.

Crazy things happened to the offspring of the grandmothers. On our block alone, we had one latent homosexual, one asexual, and three other men who were quietly retired by their families when they reached their early fifties. These three didn't work, they didn't go out, they didn't see anyone, *they didn't do anything*. They lived at home with mother — and forget that mother was in her late seventies and couldn't communicate with the outside world. Throughout the neighborhood, women would stare out at the street from their windows for days on end. The filial rejects also stared out the same windows.

No one discussed these human discards, but in each family there usually was at least one incompetent, who was unable to absorb and to cope. He never left home, while his brothers and sisters would eventually move a couple of blocks away. Since he needed to eat, the rest of the family kicked in to support him and their mother.

Where there really were conflicts were with people like Anthony, the younger generation, who saw the rejects sitting by the window and realized that there had to be something better. When the younger generation began stirring, and asking questions of the grandmothers, the old ladies dropped their balloon line of reasoning and took up with, "I want you to get a trade."

"Learning a trade" was started by the old ladies, but really pushed by people of my parents' age. Getting a trade meant that the neighborhood sent its youth to either the New York School of Printing, the New York School of Textiles, or the school that attracted most of us, Grady High School, where we were taught how to become an airplane mechanic. Grady graduated about 500 kids a year and since I was seventeen they've graduated something like 125,000 airplane mechanics, which is terrific, except that Brooklyn doesn't have 125,000 airplanes. Nor does all of New York City, for that matter.

The neighborhood airplane mechanics scaled themselves down and became garage mechanics, and those who couldn't find jobs in garages ended up in junkyards, where they were doomed to another fifty years of drudgery.

Our neighborhood did not turn out any bosses: we were not particularly strong in the rising managerial class. We still aren't today. We always worked for someone else, and took someone else's orders. If a person became a foreman, that was big news. Being a post office clerk was translated into "he's in the post office." And the implication there was that it was government, one step removed from the FBI.

During the war, mental aberrations came into vogue as the neighborhood learned that bed wetting wasn't so bad and it could be lived down — especially since chronic cases wouldn't be taken into the army. We had a lot of draft dodgers, and the years of 1941 to 1945 were the first time that the FBI ever made an appearance in the neighborhood.

All things considered, World War II was a boon to the neighborhood. It opened us up and we learned about the outside world. A few of the guys went off to war; more significantly, people in the neighborhood understood that the universe extended beyond Ocean Parkway. In 1945, when it was all over, the neighborhood celebrated. The party was not because we had won the war, since nine out of ten residents in the area did not have a clear concept of who or what Hitler and Hirohito were. Rather, we saw that everyone else was celebrating, and we figured, "Why not?"

On VJ-Day, as we threw block party after block party, we counted up our casualties and discovered that the neighborhood lost only one man — Armando Cuttinella — and that so moved us that a small park was named after him. My Uncle Freddy, our contribution to victory, conveniently missed his division's assault on Anzio. My grandfather was dying and the Red Cross got Freddy home just in time. Freddy's belongings got to Anzio but he finished up the war in Fort Campbell, Kentucky, where he picked up a lung fungus that ended up killing him ten years later.

At the end of the war, when Freddy returned from the wilds of Kentucky, all of us nervously made our way into New York City to meet him at Pennsylvania Station and stage a typical emotional outburst. He had returned from the dead, because who in the family had understood the concept of the draft? When he'd gone off to war he was written off. Nobody expected him back.

As far as the younger generation was concerned, Uncle Freddy was a world traveler. After the war he immediately slipped back into what he had been doing before he got drafted — working in a slipper factory — but I will be eternally grateful to him because he started to show me that there was another world out there. I got my first taste of Times Square with Freddy. We sat through Tommy Dorsey's Opus 1 at the Paramount Theater, and I learned about the Automat, and I saw my first fight at Madison Square Garden (Willie Pep and Sol Bartolo).

I had heard of Times Square, but hearsay never was up to the real thing. Our only entertainment, until the route to Times Square was charted, was Coney Island. It was, day and night, the entertainment center of much of Brooklyn, including our neighborhood.

Coney Island was eating out, ethnic and racial disputes, women, the whole thing. Each neighborhood would camp out on its own bay, and a bay would be a stretch of beach about two blocks wide. Bay 10 was the Italian Bay, and it was characterized by hair: curly hair, on the head and on the body. The men wore dark blue wool suits and the women wore one-piece suits. The Italians took the Sea Beach line for one stop and tumbled out of the jammed trains right onto Bay 10.

The Jewish kids walked over from Ocean Parkway and ended up in their bay, Number 7. Looking back on it all, it seems to me that the significant difference between Bay 7 and Bay 10 was body hair; we of Bay 10 were much hairier than those of Bay 7. Bays 8 and 9 were empty — literally — even on a crowded day. It looked like a mine field on Warner's back lot.

In the late 1940s and early 1950s, black residents from Brooklyn and other boroughs started to come to Coney Island. The Italian and the Jewish populations were not exactly friendly to the blacks, and territorial explosions started to take place on the perimeters of Bays 7 and 10. A friend of mine named Jimmy was stabbed during a fight protecting what he felt was his inalienable right to the joys of Bay 10.

What Brooklyn couldn't quite handle was the fact that the change occurring at the beach was taking place throughout the borough, and the fighting sometimes got very serious. The blacks and Puerto Ricans did not have any preconceived notions about Bay this or Bay that. It was hot, the water looked fine, and down they sat. Beach is beach, which is a very sensible attitude.

We also ate at Coney Island. God how we ate! I fell out of the train and fell into a couple dozen clams on the half shell. From the clams I might move on to Nathan's: hot dogs were a dime, French fries were a nickel, a large corn on the cob was a dime. Over the entire beach front wafted the sweet smell of cotton candy.

I am still addicted to clams. Once a week I'll get into my car and drive through the Brooklyn night to a vast restaurant called Lundy's at Sheepshead Bay. At the seafood bar I'll have a couple dozen fresh clams. The taste and the sea odor of the clams are fantastic, and the moment I taste the first clam I am instantly transported back to Coney Island. It was an extension of our family, our "second" home. I don't want to get overly nostalgic about the good old days, because they weren't always so good. The people weren't so good, and neither were the times. We were uneducated and frightened and very unsure of ourselves. However, there were rare times when the utter simplicity of the entire life-style worked. And I sometimes wonder why I can't have that simple goodness back again.

3

I have a non-Italian friend named Bingham who has a fixation about the Mafia. I do a lot of business with him, and we spend time together. Whenever we do any driving around the city and he spots a restaurant with a dubious past, he'll shout and say, "Hey, isn't that a Mafia joint?" Umberto's Clam Bar in Little Italy is not a Mafia joint, but Joey Gallo got himself killed there, and the killing in turn was as effective as a bad clam in casting some doubt on the restaurant in the minds of ignorant non-Italians.

If Bingham is obsessed with the Mafia, so is everyone else except the non-Mafia members of Italian descent. Most of us are bored with the Mafia. I have a Jewish colleague named Harvey who, whenever a mass killer lets loose and knocks off a dozen or so people (Richard Speck in Chicago, the guy in the college tower in Texas), prays that the mass killer is a plain old white Anglo-Saxon Protestant, not Jewish. "Thank God," says Harvey, "he's not Jewish."

This sort of thing is crazy but understandable. I yearn for the day when the reputed head of the garbage cartel is found with three bullets in the back of his head, but his name is O'Reilly. Or Epstein, for that matter.

If we didn't have many card-carrying members of the Mafia in our neighborhood, we did have many people living on the thin edge of violence. Tempers in the neighborhood were hair-trigger. For example, my earliest recollection of a wedding dates back to when I was six years old. The wedding was held in the front parlor of our house, because the bride, my mother's third cousin twice removed, didn't have any other place to go. The wedding went off nicely and I can recall sitting on the stairs outside of the parlor, away from the crowd, peacefully drinking a cream soda when suddenly a big something rolled by. That big thing was the bride's brother and he was tangled up with the groom's uncle. People were screaming for help and then someone yelled those magic words, "My God, watch out, he's got a knife!" Well, that tore it, because it wasn't proper to bring a knife to a family wedding, and when word of the knife was shouted, the entire wedding piled on. They untangled the uncle and the brother, found no knife, made everyone grudgingly shake hands, and the wedding went on about its business. My point being that no one was overly shocked about the possibility that a knife *was* there; my parents simply didn't want any strange, third-cousin's blood on the rug.

We had an abundance of people like the late Joey Gielli. I played ball with Joey, who was about seven years older than I was. He was short, fat, and his hair was always slicked back. He also was a full-fledged, practicing psychopath. To give you a random example: one day I heard a commotion out on West Seventh Street — I couldn't have been more than fifteen years old at the time — and there on the street lay a guy with his head split open and blood flowing. What had happened was that Gielli had stopped his car to talk with a girl. Since West Seventh Street was very narrow, he blocked traffic. The car behind Gielli honked its horn. Gielli yelled, "Wait a minute, dummy." Dummy hadn't waited a minute but had blown his horn again, longer than before. Gielli calmly reached under his seat for a lug wrench, got out of his car, and caved the guy's head in.

I suppose the fellow survived. Gielli didn't panic; he kept talking to the girl until he was finished saying what he had to say, and then drove off. The motorist behind the guy who got slugged didn't say a word.

Although Gielli wasn't exactly *one* of us, he was around. You'd see him at the candy store; around the schoolyard he was a presence. We were wary of him because we knew he was capable of killing. He married a girl from the neighborhood, so I knew him well enough to say hello; but nothing more than that. When he played ball with us, we always listened very carefully to his decisions on close calls. For example, if Gielli said a guy was safe at second you could assume that he was safe at second.

One day a friend of mine named Frankie got into a fight with Gielli. They fought for about fifteen minutes and beat the hell out of each other. When it was all over, my friend Frankie did a very smart thing: he disappeared. He simply left the neighborhood, just got the hell out of there.

We used to talk about Gielli because we always knew he was full-fledged Mafia or close to it. We found out for certain years later during the Gallo-Profaci war. On the outbreak of hostilities, he was the first guy killed, for which he achieved considerable notoriety. He was taken out on a boat and never returned. His clothes were wrapped around a large dead fish and the fish was left on his widow's front doorstep in the neighborhood.

Today, Gielli is credited, in the same books, with having been the point man in the contract killing of Albert Anastasia, who, as you may remember, was murdered in a barber's chair while enjoying a shave and a haircut in the old Park Sheraton Hotel in New York City.

Mostly, organized crime, that favorite subject of newspapers and magazines, was not a subject that we really knew much about. Although the Mafia was never mentioned in my household, we were all aware of it. A few blocks from our house lived one of the organization's grand old men, Carlo Gambino, who died last year. If you didn't know that his house was on the corner of Ocean Parkway and Avenue U, you could always figure it out because the FBI unmarked van kept Gambino under surveillance from across the street until the day he died.

I was born on the north side of West Seventh Street and then moved to the south side of the street when I was a child. In the grand scheme of the neighborhood, West Seventh Street was "good," which meant that although we might have (and we did) an occasional criminal (or an occasional "He's away for a while" situation), we didn't have out-and-out shooting in the streets.

When we reached junior high school we began to break the rules. But I could begin to see the difference even then:

some of us were breaking the rules and some of us were breaking the law. A group of us who were not into active lawbreaking had stumbled across a truck that was partially hidden in one of the innumerable dumps around the neighborhood. No one was going to find that truck deliberately unless they knew exactly where it was.

The truckload of radio tubes originally had been hijacked by a gang of guys who lived on West Tenth, West Eleventh, West Twelfth, and West Thirteenth Streets and Avenue U. *They* were regarded as the crazy ones in the neighborhood, hotheaded enough to go out with guns and masks and force the driver of a truck to turn over thousands of dollars' worth of radio tubes to them.

When we came across the tubes we figured that whoever had hijacked the truck did not know what they were stealing. They left the tubes sitting on the truck until they could find out how to fence them. The lot number of the tubes was 5 U4 and there they were, thousands of radio tubes, in a neighborhood where there weren't that many radios. Each of us carted away some tubes and then we were stuck with them. They hung around our cellars for months until one Halloween we used them as noisy hand grenades, tossing them against lampposts and on the streets.

At the age of fifteen, we were a bit frightened of what we were doing when we took the tubes. It was a two-way thing: we knew that what we were up to was strictly illegal; and we knew that if the guys who had done the original stealing ever caught up with us, we would be in very deep trouble. They would not be hampered at all by any moral restraints; if they had to kill us to make a point, they would.

Four blocks away from fairly straight West Seventh,

things were much worse. West Tenth was a very tough street and the four-block difference in criminal intent had more to do with geographic origin than it did with family income. We all were poor, but West Seventh Street was more Neapolitan and West Tenth was strictly Sicilian. The immigrants from Sicily brought with them closer contact and knowledge of the Mafia while people leaving Naples simply did not have the exposure (or the involvement). It was this elementary geography more than anything else that colored the neighborhood's attitude toward law and order.

The toughest kids hung around one particular candy store on West Tenth Street, called the Rat Hole. It's still there, although it has been boarded up for years. If we had a potential cop-killer growing up on West Seventh Street, he wouldn't hang around our candy store — you'd find him lounging at the Rat Hole. When the kids in the neighborhood realized that the crew on West Tenth was truly dangerous, we went out of our way to avoid them. My candy store was on Macdonald Avenue and I stayed there for years, never venturing into the Rat Hole.

The violence in the West Tenth Street area spread into all aspects of life. Even the bar owners were not immune. A man named Jerry who owned the hangout bar on the block eventually ended up with his head blown off, stuffed in the trunk of his expensive Cadillac. As things turned out, his body was just the first in a series and for a while the cops were turning up a dead hoodlum a week. One Mafia family had simply decided to clean house and get rid of a lot of marginal members. The *Daily News* made a big thing out of it by calling it a gangland war, but the neighborhood knew otherwise.

The cops were all over Gravesend as they occasionally were when more than one body was found within a month's time. The whole neighborhood was questioned during the investigation of Jerry's death by plainclothesmen, wondering if we knew anything.

All of the "connected" guys drove Cadillacs. They didn't wear pinky rings but they were dressed better than anyone else. When a connected guy was expected in the neighborhood on Avenue U — there would be a sudden awareness that *he* was coming — no one would know precisely how this information was received, except that it was always accurate.

Soon a flashy car would drive up, and the soldier of the local family would emerge. He'd be dressed simply — white shirt, pair of dark slacks, jacket — and usually he would conduct his business with someone very quietly near the candy store. That seemed to be very important, somehow, because in all of these comings and goings I never saw any of the wise guys go *into* the candy store. They always talked *near* the store. At a safe distance, the neighborhood watched with avid curiosity. All of the gamblers, the bust-out guys, the hangers-on, the potential hoods, the kids desperately wanting to become connected were trying to stay cool and unconcerned but they were watching. After all, this was our version of royalty.

The only thing of value I took with me into the real world after living *through* my neighborhood was the ability to spot instantly in a crowd who really holds the power. I learned this from watching how the true Mafia guys would conduct themselves and how we would identify them. It is the same thing as going into a corporation boardroom and wondering who the leader of the company is. Whom do you have to win over? Today, if I meet with five or six men, I can spot the individual who *pretends* to have the power, and I also can immediately perceive who truly *is* the strength behind the pretender. It is exactly how things were when I grew up. You knew almost at once who were the blowhards, the story-tellers, the braggarts, and who had the clout. The true Mafia guys had a way about them; they walked differently, they carried themselves with a certain confidence that the ordinary punks in the neighborhood just didn't have.

The worst crime ever to occur in Gravesend was the non-Mafia killing of two cops in 1958. Two detectives happened to be walking on West Eleventh Street near Highland Avenue, and one of them decided he needed a pack of cigarettes. They walked into a tobacco shop and smack into the middle of a holdup conducted by a kid named Franco and a Jewish kid from the other side of Ocean Parkway named Klein. Franco and Klein were told by the cops to get their hands up and get out on the sidewalk. Franco then copied what he had seen in a movie the night before. He dropped his gun on the sidewalk and raised his hands. He let one cop pass him by but as soon as the cop had passed abreast of him, he quickly picked up the gun and shot the first cop in the back and killed him. The second cop was blinded by the sun and in that terrible instant Franco shot him dead and ran.

Cops swarmed into our neighborhood in numbers like we had never seen before. Kids were rousted out of their social clubs and out of their homes. And a lot of guys got the hell beat out of them in the police's search for information. A guy named Lefty, one of the twenty or so hoods who hung around the Rat Hole, knew where Franco had gone to ground. The cops broke his nose, his jaw, and one of his arms, and Lefty decided enough was enough and he told them where they could find Franco, which they eventually did.

Franco died in Attica about ten years ago. Klein is still in jail. Franco's mother lives in the neighborhood and still wears black. She still believes that her boy was framed. The motto on every Italian woman's breast is: "He's a good boy." Franco's mother claims that he happened to be taking a ride with a couple of true bums and *they* were intending to do something terrible. Franco, she says, didn't know anything about it and when the others started to rob the tobacco store her Franco was just sitting out in that car not knowing what was going on. The shooting took place, Klein ran away, and her Franco was the fall guy. Until Franco died his mother was always talking of how he was going to be home soon and she was planning a big party for him. By the way, in Franco's family are a number of very law-abiding citizens, including a good friend of mine who is a cop.

I know that the maniacs over on West Tenth Street were continually trying to bring the old country with them. The Sicilians truly *believed* and were ready to go out and kill if someone talked the wrong way to one of their sisters. Their standards were fairly simple: whatever worked in Italy would work over here, even if that included family vendettas, kidnapings for honor, and so on.

What always staggered me was that we brought the violence along with us, *generation after generation* — it wasn't one of these happenstance things. In a horrible way, this country was perfectly suited for the Sicilian *fix* on things. The poor Sicilian had to cope with the same lousy institutions he had in the old country: the Church, the army, a civil service bureaucracy. The only things unfamiliar to him were the language barrier and the schools — and he didn't pay much attention to either of those.

We had no northern Italians in our neighborhood. The Milanese simply stayed the hell home: arrogant, smug, holier-than-thou. What did they need with the United States? I'm quite sure that if a Milanese would deign to take a trip to the New World to see how the southern Italian immigrants were doing, he would return with, "Jesus, they're living like dogs."

In the 1930s and the 1940s and even in the 1950s, we were the blacks of our time. In many respects it was an image self-inflicted and we liked it: fantastic shoemakers, even better custom tailors, terrific boxers, sensational restaurateurs, and equally sensational baseball players. We were — the black population will kindly forgive me — the first people to have natural rhythm ascribed to us and the first people to have natural athletic ability as well. "Look at that Italian kid box!" And, "Hey, these people sure do know how to sing! Have you ever heard anything like Sinatra, Tony Bennett, etc.?"

On top of this we also were known as the world's natural gangsters, the best hoodlums of all time, the creators of that terrific secret society the Mafia, which kept the movie industry going in hard times. As a result of typecasting, Italians as a group sat down and said, "Well, fuck it, if that's what they want then that's what we'll give them." So we laughed and we sang and we served a hell of a zabaglione and then, behind everyone's back, we told stories in strange dialects that no one from Milan would ever understand.

The sad thing about the sixteen- and seventeen-year-olds who desperately wanted to become members of the Mafia was that few if any were ultimately chosen. The Mafia was not dumb; it didn't want most of the half-baked crazies who were posing over on West Tenth Street. Those who were too dumb for the Mafia never saw the light of day at home, on their twentieth birthday: they usually were in jail someplace, or on the run.

About two years ago, I was walking up Park Avenue and I passed a construction site. It was a bitter cold day and suddenly I looked at one of the workers leaning on his shovel and recognized him as a guy from the neighborhood, Billy. I always knew that Billy was slated for jail from the moment he was born: I just didn't know exactly when he was going.

I met him in the eighth grade and watched him punch out a number of teachers. I saw him going through boats in the Sheepshead Bay Marina, ripping off whatever he could find. And then one day I opened up the *Daily News* and found him on page 2, lying on Stillwell Avenue under the Elevated, with a broken leg. The broken leg he got from his car, which crashed. His car crashed because the cops were chasing him at 70 miles an hour. In his car was $60,000 worth of hot jewels. He'd just robbed a jeweler and because he was so astonishingly stupid he tripped the silent alarm. Thus the cops, therefore the chase, and that's why the seven and a half to fifteen years for armed robbery. And then I didn't see him until that day on Park Avenue when I spotted him. I don't think he saw me; at least I hope he didn't. I'm sure he's going to be back in again; it's just a matter of time.

The kids in Gravesend couldn't have figured out a big-time swindle or scam. They were content with trying to stick up gas stations or stores — all outside of the neighborhood. They didn't commit any violent crimes like mugging or rape. And they sure weren't sophisticated enough to rob a bank, plan the thing from its inception. The Mafia wanted more sophisticated criminals than someone who could only rob an occasional jewelry store. They shied away from banks because banks had a multiplicity of alarms and guards with guns, and a lot of people around who could yell for help.

The schools also had a hand in nurturing crime. In junior high school, when children from different streets came together for the first time, the school system separated everyone according to I.Q. Thus, all of the psychotics, potential psychotics, and guys from the Rat Hole were thrown in together and it was practically a self-fulfilling prophecy that they would end up bent. I suppose some genius at the Board of Education felt much better seeing them all under one roof.

I can't give a rational explanation as to why some of us went straight, some went into small-time crime, and a very few made it all the way into the Mob. We were all listening to the same vowels and consonants. We all heard the same oral history, passed on from one family member to another. I don't buy the bad-seed theory; we all had essentially the same blood. And I have trouble in believing that the environment was totally to blame, because we all had the same surroundings. Our parents were alike, and I swear that the economic situation of one family could not have been separated by more than forty bucks a year in total income from that of any other family. All of us were poor. And yet there you have it: West Seventh, fairly law-abiding; and West Tenth, maniacs and killers and desperadoes looking for someplace new to hold up every night.

The guys who began hanging around the Rat Hole and then graduated to bars were in one sense a gang, but in another sense not. They had no specific leaders and they surely didn't wear phony gang jackets. But they had guns by the age of sixteen, and they knew how to use them. Pseudo-tough guys (and I include myself) were the jacket wearers. But the boys on West Tenth at a very early age were professional enough to know that they didn't want to be easily identified.

The entire group on West Tenth Street served time. It might have been a short term but each guy who hung out on that street eventually ended up with a police record. It was almost like a tough town out West, but in that tough town there was one particular saloon which was the toughest of them all.

The Mafia was in the neighborhood and then it wasn't. There were no signs nor were there any arrows pointing: "This way to the Mafia." Today, when I go over to Brooklyn and drive up and down Avenue U, I see the private social clubs and wonder who is or who isn't a member. Not long ago a tipster called the cops and reported that there had been a shooting and a murder in a social club on Avenue U.

Five cars full of gun-toting cops arrived at the social club and found a few tired-looking old men sitting around drinking evil-looking coffee and playing pinochle. The cops were about to leave when one of them happened to notice that one of the walls was liberally sprayed with fresh blood. Sure enough, three blocks away in a vacant lot, a body miraculously appeared. No one at the social club could even guess how the blood got on the wall.

I am unable to point to one specific person in the neighborhood and say, "Yes, I am sure that this guy is connected. He's a soldier in the Profaci Family, or a button man in the Gallo Family." I don't know; neither do the rest of the citizens. This is the way the Mafia wants it and, believe me, it is exactly how the straight citizens want it. We don't want to be privy to *any* knowledge about the Mob; let the cops go and solve it but count us out. And although our neighborhood had traditionally been the turf of the Profacis, in recent years the Gallos tried to make inroads and this led to a still further increase in business for the funeral homes. My parents, by the way, deny totally the existence of any crime whatsoever in a twenty-block radius of our home. If you were to say, "Hey, what are all of these bodies doing falling out of the trees?" they'd only look at you and ask, "What bodies?" It goes without saying that they've never heard a word about the Mafia in forty years.

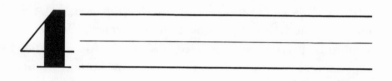

Forgetting the Mafia, plain old law and order was a rather difficult concept for Avenue U. Ask any resident of the neighborhood today what "law and order" is and it's a probable eight to five he won't know. In the next breath mention that some interesting goods have just arrived at a neighbor's house and if this fellow is interested in a size 42 brown cashmere overcoat for $65.00, no questions asked or state sales tax to bother with, watch his response.

It was quite possible that suddenly, in an obscure neighborhood of Brooklyn, a hundred and forty men would turn up wearing the same brown cashmere overcoat, size 42, in fact the same lot number from one of the manufacturers who supplied Brooks Brothers with brown cashmere overcoats. We didn't find this overcoat cloudburst unusual, and we won't in the future. The coats simply fell off the truck.

On one famous occasion — absolutely true, I swear to God — I could have walked into three hundred homes in my neighborhood, gone into the three hundred bathrooms, looked at the three hundred toilets, and suddenly discovered three hundred identical toilet-seat covers (plastic jobs, dainty pink), which happened to be that week's "special." My own family's pink cover just wore out a few years ago.

Growing up as we did, we immediately understood if someone in the household casually mentioned that some tennis balls were available; we realized that one hell of a lot of tennis balls had just fallen off a truck.

There wasn't a tennis racquet among us — in fact I truly didn't know anything beyond baseball and the horses — but if tennis balls were hot, why not pick up a few?

The entire neighborhood did not steal. My parents, for example, were never seen loitering around the docks. But they certainly availed themselves of whatever might be for sale at any given time.

There was one family on my block, the Gambrellis, who were in various businesses during my growing up. They were the first in the neighborhood to introduce many people to penicillin. On another occasion we got a knock on the door and were politely asked by a Gambrelli if we were interested in size 10 women's summer dresses. This was in the dead of January.

Although only a handful of people were suppliers, all of us bought. The world cannot resist a bargain, and we were no exception. Although I wasn't sure of the Gambrellis' source of supply, I did know for a fact that two older members worked on the docks. I might be sitting home one night listening to the radio, not doing much, when there would be a knock on the door. It might be a Gambrelli asking if any Della Feminas would like to buy a hundred Columbia girls' bikes — quickly and cheaply. These people dealt in volume.

Those in the neighborhood who happened to be on the street when the cartons fell didn't need to be told about Newton and the laws of gravity; on Avenue U the law of gravity was demonstrated when a thousand size 36 green sweaters landed on the corner. I do not believe that any Italian who grew up in Brooklyn around the 1940s and 1950s wasn't aware of hot goods; and everyone participated in it.

The line between legitimate and illegitimate was drawn the moment the stuff hit the pavement. On the street it was okay and we all participated. Of course it was a random-sample kind of affair. Not only did we not play tennis, nine out of ten residents of the neighborhood did not know what tennis was. Thus, when ten thousand tennis balls came rolling our way, we didn't know what the hell to do with them.

The point to remember is that buying hot goods was so ingrained that no one thought it wrong, immoral, or against the law. There were few outside mores reaching our neighborhood. Consequently, the neighborhood did not know that the rest of the world thought trafficking in hot goods was illegal.

The news of a shipment spread quickly. I can remember guys coming around the house flashing a suit saying, "Look. We're going to come in and show you all of the suits at

once. Get your family and friends in at the same time."
It was a sort of Avon Lady party of our day. While my
friend was making arrangements for people to come in for
a suit, we weren't sitting around making moral judgments
that this is buying stolen goods and it's wrong. Rather it
was, How are we going to get Cousin Ralph (who weighed
maybe 250 pounds) into a size 40 suit? The guy selling
the stuff didn't care how it looked; he was interested in
speedy disposal. "I got four 38's, four 32's, four 40's, and
listen, Ralph, all you got to do is let the seams out a bit
on this here 40 and it'll fit you like a glove." Ralph, who
didn't own anything that fit him anyhow and of course
didn't give a damn how he looked, usually bought the suit
for twenty bucks and that was that. A bargain is a bargain.

Incidentally, there were no checks, no credit cards, no
charge accounts. Cash on the line. The "salesmen" never
had any credit problems.

My family shopped regularly from the Gambrellis and
never thought about it. One spring a truckload of iridescent
green jackets hit the streets and I got one. It took me until
the age of sixteen, when I got to the outside world, to realize
that the whole business was wrong. Today, my mother has
(reluctantly) quit shopping from the Gambrellis, because
she's afraid of what I might say. She'll show me something
she's bought and my first question is, "Is it hot?" Her
answer always is, "Don't be silly, you know we don't do
that kind of thing anymore."

Well, my mother may not be doing it anymore but the
neighborhood is very much like an old dog, still crazy
about old tricks. Of course people get sophisticated. I was
sitting around the local candy store a few months ago
and heard a fragment of conversation about some "im-

ported stuff." In the old days "Made in the U.S.A." was enough of a label for the locals; nowadays their tastes are jaded.

During the Christmas shopping season, some neighborhood guys would drive within a block or two of a department store, park, take off their coats, put a pencil behind the ear, and freeze their asses off for a block and a half walking to the store. Then they'd step right onto the loading docks, grab a loaded dolly, and walk right out to their cars with a load of goods. Other of my friends, who were cuter, would go to the garment center in Manhattan and head for a manufacturer of cheap clothing. They would buy a hundred suits for twenty dollars apiece and then, back in the neighborhood, they'd take people around to the car, open the trunk and flash the suits, and then mark up the price by twenty or thirty dollars. If anything, the neighborhood was consistent; everyone loved a bargain and usually the suits would be sold without difficulty.

What I've always loved about hot goods was the fantastic variety and the surprise of it all. One Christmas, when I was home with my family, a friend named Willie seriously asked me if I wanted three dozen sinks, complete with hot and cold faucets. It never occurred to Willie that I might not be a plumbing subcontractor. He had some goods that had taken a tumble from a truck and he was offering them to a friend for a price.

Morality never made inroads in the hot-goods traffic. But container shipping sure as hell did. When containerized shipping was introduced back in the late 1950s, hot goods began to take a beating. The whole concept of containerized *anything* set back the Italian household tremendously.

In some respects it was like the frontier. The neighborhood had its own moral code. Stealing from your next-door neighbor was never allowed. Stealing from the outside world (if it was done without a gun) was perfectly legitimate. Many of the longshoremen who came from the neighborhood worked like animals in an environment (the docks) that was totally corrupt. From the moment they went to the morning shape-up, which was corrupt, to the minute they got home in the evening, they were surrounded by corruption. And they were very simplistic in their attitude: they felt that the world owed them something beyond a ruined back after forty years of labor. If a thousand scarves happened to be in a carton and the guy thought he could get it off the docks and into his car without too much trouble, he did it.

I have a friend named Howie, who also grew up in Brooklyn, who says that his neighborhood was so sophisticated that if you were interested in a particular make of car, it would be stolen for you right down to the correct color. We never had anything like that when I was growing up. What we had — and still have — are an inordinate number of auto wreckers. They're all on Cropsie Avenue: at least two dozen of them. We're a neighborhood of AUTO WRECKING and COLLISION WORK signs. Each one of the wreckers is guarded by six or seven giant, mangy brown dogs. Periodically, there is a police investigation of the entire auto-wrecking industry in Brooklyn (not just Cropsie Avenue). I can remember the *News* hinting that the Mafia occasionally had a piece of an auto wrecker.

All auto wreckers seem to own one of those giant pulverizers that can take a car and compact it into a small package of solid metal, which is then recycled into a range of items, including women's jewelry. I happen to believe that the Mafia occasionally would dump a stiff into the trunk of a car, take the car to an auto wrecker, and then have the car compacted. I also feel it is conceivable that someone could end up wearing an earring composed of a 1952 Chevy and a mobster named Big Tony.

If hot merchandise was one integral part of our life, then gambling was the other. The whole neighborhood bet as much as they bought hot goods, and when the City of New York announced with fanfare that they were introducing something called Off Track Betting to the world, my Uncle Pete could not grasp that he would be going to a city-run parlor rather than a candy store. He still bets with the bookie, studiously avoiding the Avenue U OTB.

Betting was a way of life, and the bookmaker was a well-known and respected member of the community. When high school graduation was held it was assumed that the toughest kid in the class would eventually go into the Mafia. The weakest member of the class became a hooked bettor.

Being the toughest kid in the class did not necessarily mean that he was the smartest, which is why the Mafia didn't always get the pick of the crop.

Bookmaking was always conducted at the candy store. Craps was everywhere, especially on Sunday, right out in front of a cigar store on Avenue U. There was always a big crowd, and despite an occasional police charge a lot of money used to change hands.

Craps was the game of the young bloods; horses the sport of all of us. And the old Italians sat all day long in front of their houses playing a game like three-card monte, called Brisk. Brisk is to Italians what gin rummy is to Jews.

If a kid showed an aptitude for numbers, he started shooting craps at the age of thirteen or fourteen. I was about fifteen when I began. In some of the games hundreds of dollars were at stake, but for the most part the swing ran to about forty or fifty dollars. We never had a problem with bad dice or cheating because outsiders were not allowed in.

The bookies of the neighborhood formed a part of the upper strata of our society, and as such they only would participate in the bigger crap games. Often they'd be called in for what might be considered binding arbitration or to settle a jurisdictional dispute.

The neighborhood had about fifteen bookies in it, which worked out to about one bookie for every three blocks. None of the bookies was Mob, but obviously they all had connections for heavy layoffs if they needed it. We needed fifteen bookies, frankly, because there was one hell of a lot of business in that neighborhood.

I used to have a friend named Charlie who had been a superb athlete; he had been such a promising ball player that he had tried out for the Dodgers as a kid. Although he never made the team, he became entranced with betting on baseball and the team he fell in love with was the Dodgers. He loved them, but they didn't return the sentiment because Charlie lost thousands. He kept betting, losing, doubling up, losing, tripling up, losing, and so on. Finally, he got in so deep that he robbed a grocery store and got caught for that and sent away for four years. At prison he played on the baseball team.

He got out, returned to the neighborhood, and started betting on the Dodgers again, went broke again, robbed another grocery store, got sent back to prison. Once Charlie got very sick and I saw his bookie on Charlie's block, carrying a large bowl and actually heading for the guy's house. "Where you going?" I asked the bookie, fearing for Charlie's life. "I got some soup for him, maybe it will make him feel better," the bookie said, and he meant it. He had a real stake in Charlie's health.

One day, Charlie was walking down a narrow street — actually a cul-de-sac — a friend of Charlie's spotted him from the rear and yelled out his name. That so frightened Charlie that he dived immediately into the bushes lining the street. He thought that the bookies had finally come to do him in.

Although it is easy to make gambling and bookmaking and the whole business sound like a Brooklyn version of *Guys and Dolls,* there was a dark and horrible side to it. Charlie's fear was one aspect of it. The other aspect was the actual violence the bookies sometimes unleashed. When I was fourteen I witnessed a scene that has never left me: Al, a compulsive gambler, had been hooked beyond hope. He had reached a point of being in the hole with the bookies that they had to punish him for two reasons: (1) to save face to the neighborhood; and (2) to try to get some of their money back. Actually, the bookies had to show the neighborhood every once in a while that they meant business, and it was Al's misfortune to be the example.

Two hoods were hired by the bookie to teach Al the lesson. A bunch of us kids were sitting around a local park when the two guys caught up with Al. They knew Al, played ball with Al, and now it was time to beat the hell out of Al. They did it with tire chains, and as we watched

— too petrified to move or even to talk — they deliberately broke his legs with the chains. One guy held Al, and the other guy swung the chains with all his might and just broke his legs.

Al didn't make a sound. He knew what was going on and in a strange way he knew he was lucky: the bookie had decided not to have him killed. We were the audience, and the beating was done right out in the open because the bookie knew that anyone who saw the beating would spread the word. In this manner the bookie got the idea across graphically that it was not safe to get in too deep with the books.

Bookies who stayed bookies usually lived to fairly ripe old ages. Bookies who got overly ambitious and wanted to further their criminal careers ran into trouble from the real Mafia.

Another guy from the neighborhood was a bookie and also a bit of a loan shark. He dressed sharply, always drove a late-model Cadillac, and met his Maker in a most embarrassing fashion. He died in bed, which is every bookie's dream. Unfortunately, it wasn't his bed and the lady wasn't his wife.

Bookies *always* came from the neighborhood. In their youth they always were a little sharper than the others, always a bit impatient, always a little superior. It wasn't as if they showed any particular academic aptitude. Their real strength was in their relationships with people. A good bookie, even at that early age, showed a certain amount of magnetism. He was popular with people, he demonstrated leadership. People would listen to him, and he could persuade people to do as he suggested. Bookies were *nice*, they could be charming. Obviously, they had enough sense of self-preservation to have someone's legs broken with a chain. There is niceness and there is niceness.

A kid would almost automatically gravitate toward bookmaking and the Mob element in the community would spot the comers and quietly offer encouragement. Ours was a neighborhood that needed a certain number of bookies to survive. They were an essential service, just like sanitation, or Con Ed, or telephones.

After a few years as a bookie, the young guys would take on the appearance of the older guys. Although their hair might not have changed to silver-gray, they all dressed very sharply. They all drove Buicks or Cadillacs. They all talked with a supreme air of confidence. I was born in the Depression and grew up through several recessions. The bookies never faltered. They always had their Cadillacs; they always were looked up to. Bookies only got into trouble when they were poaching on the Mob's turf. Although somebody in the organization might have said, "Yeah, this kid has the makings of a bookie, let him alone," the organization would quickly withdraw that support if the bookie got ambitious in other areas of crime.

I spent my childhood arguing about Italian ball players: DiMaggio, Rizzuto, Berra. And, logically, most of the action in betting was baseball and the horses. No one bet football because in those days we only knew about college football and nobody cared. (There was little, if any, betting on pro football.) The neighborhood was terribly suspicious about anyone who went to college. Naturally, they didn't want to wager any money on something coming out of college — like football. We were big on boxing, and I can remember lining up in a block-long queue on Lake

Street for the first Floyd Patterson–Ingemar Johansson fight. The whole neighborhood felt that Patterson was a stiff and we all bet on Johansson and won.

The neighborhood gambled because gambling was hope. We didn't play the numbers; the blacks had that concession up in Harlem. The neighborhood didn't say to itself, "Tomorrow I'm going to get a better job"; they weren't looking for better jobs. The neighborhood was really saying, "Tomorrow that tip on the horse in the third at Aqueduct is going to come in." We wanted to believe that the races were fixed, that the game was fixed, that the fight was fixed. Every deal, every bet, everything we ever touched had to be "hot" in one way or another.

Since we were operating on a paranoid frequency that the world was fixed and if we had word of the fix we'd be a winner, we ended up betting on anything that was running. We bet every day except Sunday, and on Sunday we bet on dice. Our neighborhood was composed of garbage carriers, dock guys, shipping clerks, post office guys, and from Monday through Friday the bosses of the world leaned on the clerks of the world and made them feel like dirt. Although I might be a lowly clerk on Thursday I could have a tip on a horse named Elliot's Dream in the third at Aqueduct on Saturday, and this gave me a feeling of considerable power over my boss. That tip, coming from the second cousin of an Aqueduct groom, gave the neighborhood an exhilarating feeling. Our tips made us big, made us feel important, lifted us out of our daily frustrations. We didn't make any decisions worth a damn during the week, but by God we were all backing Elliot's Dream on Saturday, and that was our decision.

I remember once when the entire neighborhood — and

I mean everyone, including the local priest, who gave us the tip — was on a horse named Manassah Mauler. The important thing was that the horse was owned by an Italian, trained by an Italian, and ridden by a jockey named Mike Salamone. We all were in on this at sixty to one.

On that day of Manassah Mauler, a young but rising bookie named Nunzio was doing a fantastic business. The local candy store was near the schoolyard where we all played ball, but everyone was headed to get their bets in. Lower-echelon Mafia had decided that Nunzio could handle that particular street and candy store and now young guys were coming in at him in waves. He'd walk out of the candy store every once in a while, go to the bar and make a phone call laying off the action, and then get back to the candy store to take more bets.

God was keeping an eye on us because the damned horse came in at something like fifty to one. And we all hit. Although it would go down in neighborhood legend as one of the great fixed races of all time, it wasn't so. What probably happened was that the trainer told someone that his horse finally was ready to go. The trainer probably had been holding him back for the past five or six races to get a price on him. And that day finally arrived.

I can remember one tip — around 1955 — on a trotter that was running at Roosevelt Raceway, a horse by the name of Volo Yates. I owned an ancient Mercury that was falling apart. Four of us piled into the Mercury and set off on the Belt Parkway at seventy miles an hour to make Roosevelt Raceway in time to cash in on the fabulous tip. Everyone else from the neighborhood was also flying out there. The bookies evidently had been warned about the race and weren't taking any bets on it.

When we finally got out to Roosevelt we had exactly six dollars in our pockets after paying admission. Volo Yates was running in the fourth, and we had a horrendous decision. We were in time for the third race and what do we do, bet two dollars on the third leaving four dollars for the fourth? Or do we lay off the third and plunge everything on Volo Yates?

I blew two dollars on the third, leaving only four dollars on the fourth. That race was more than twenty years ago, but I'll never forget it. Volo Yates was fifth coming down the stretch and none of the horses was moving. And Volo Yates, who hadn't won a race in twenty-four starts, started to move. Up to fourth, then to third. We were screaming and going berserk, but fifty yards from the finish he was stuck behind horses one and two and there was no way he could go between them and win.

And then, as my friend described it, the gates of heaven opened and Volo Yates went right through them. It was as if one of the drivers said to the other, "Let the stiff through." He burst right through the middle, won, and paid eighty-two dollars, and we were laughing, crying, and kissing each other. And in the time-honored tradition of bettors we also were saying, "Why didn't we put more on the horse?"

Did we go home after this triumph and save the money for another day? Of course not. We acted like big shots, hung around the track, and then blew the money, ending up with about fifteen dollars profit among us.

Roosevelt Raceway was an hour away, Jamaica and Aqueduct less than an hour's drive. We'd sometimes drive out for the last race because they'd throw open the admission gates then and we could get in and save the two-dollar entry fee. Everybody would run in, make a bet on the last race, and go home again. In the fall when we'd make the drive, sometimes we'd have to wait out in the parking lot in the cold until the last race. We might be freezing but it didn't occur to any of us that it didn't make any sense to do it. We were that hooked.

We all faithfully believed that a bettor never ever wins completely; there always is a piece of bad news coming down the pike to let him have it in the teeth. If I won at the track, I really expected my car to break down.

There wasn't a kid in the neighborhood who didn't believe this tit-for-tat philosophy. We may not have had any religious credence, but we certainly felt that there was some force afoot to balance any luck we might have had. Something good has happened — hold your breath, here comes the bad.

We were a population of poor devils who would go to Aqueduct during the day and get killed, and then take the bus over to the trotters at Roosevelt, get killed again, and then take the losers' bus home.

The literature of the neighborhood consisted of the *Daily Racing Form* and the *Morning Telegraph,* and our national heroes were Ken Kling and Joe Gelardi of the *Daily Mirror.* In many neighborhoods people might have been talking about what books they'd read recently. In my neighborhood we'd be talking about the latest Joe and Asbestos column.

"Joe and Asbestos," the Kling cartoon strip, predicted through a code the winner of the next day's feature race at a New York track. Within the dialogue of Joe and Asbestos was the code. However, the code meant nothing unless the reader had bought a Joe and Asbestos key, which was available at local newsstands for fifty cents. At the age of fifteen I saved old issues of the *Mirror* and in a month I had figured out the code, making me a hero in the neighborhood.

My father played the horses; my uncle was a tremendous gambler; the whole neighborhood was into horses. Going to the track was not a lonely business; everybody was there. I knew a young fellow named Ray who went to the track twenty-four times in a row and came back with a new car each time. Ray realized that the best place to steal a car was at the track. He'd come back to the neighborhood each day with his stolen car and either get rid of the entire car or sell it off piece by piece to the junkyard: here a fender, there a transmission. Eventually, Ray stole the wrong car, or said the wrong thing, or talked to the wrong people, because at the age of eighteen he got himself fatally shot up. People raised an eyebrow when Ray got killed, but that was about it, except for his immediate family.

Bodies were constantly being discovered in our neighborhood, guys were constantly being killed. Neighbors were leaving for prison and coming back. We didn't produce anything except robbery and gambling and fencing and hot goods. And nobody second-guessed us. No one ever asked why I was going to the track for the nineteenth day in a row.

Along with everything else, there was a common loser's attitude in the neighborhood, whether in gambling or anything else. A guy would walk around saying, "I got to go with Cincinnati tonight against the Phillies even though I know that the God of baseball is going to decide that

[Ewell "The Whip"] Blackwell is going to come up with a sore elbow and be pulled from the starting rotation." Or he might say, "I got to bet the three horse even though I know he can't run in the mud and it looks like it's going to rain today." We lost every way you can imagine. We lost in photo finishes — we were a neighborhood of lost photo finishes. The dice got cold, the Dodgers got cold, Eddie Arcaro, the patron saint of Italian horseplayers, got cold.

We were a people who always had to catch up, double up, make up our losses. If I got wiped out at Belmont during the summer, I bet Hialeah in the fall. If we treated our bookies with respect, it was because in the fall we had no action; we had to bet out of town. Our bookie was the lifeline to exotic places such as Gulfstream, Hollywood Park, Santa Anita.

But our lives — especially the dedicated gamblers' lives — were empty. One guy I grew up with, Dom, learned gambling at an early age and got hooked terribly. He worked mornings at the vegetable market, and he went out to the track every day, moving over to the trotters every night. He's still in the neighborhood, but he's a prisoner of the neighborhood and his gambling. He never married; he lives at home, at the age of fifty, with his elderly parents and plays the horses.

There sometimes is a wife in all of this. And if the man is a desperate character, I don't even know where to begin to describe the woman. She is more of a victim than the man. Needless to say, she is always left behind. She stays at home during the crap game, the night at the races, the basketball game. That is man's business. I know one woman, Tina, so poor that she had to go to her father's home and beg for food money. She did without new clothes, new shoes. But Tina can't complain, nor is she allowed to contemplate divorce. There can be no divorce; the word and the concept are unknown. The priest had told Tina that there is no reason to leave Bob, her husband. None, short of murder. Adultery, brutality, gambling, nonproviding, all of that came with the territory. Just because her husband lost everything at the races was no reason to complain. She simply picked a bad apple.

The thing about the neighborhood, and the gambling, and the crime, and the way we lived, is this: we didn't live in New York City. We never *saw* New York City; we only *saw* selected areas of Brooklyn. Any real traveling we did was in connection with gambling. We traveled into Queens to play the flats at Jamaica and Aqueduct. That wasn't Manhattan, which frightened us a little. We didn't do anything of consequence except gamble, especially during the summer.

Gambling really began in early June, when school let out, and it went through the entire summer and into fall. Gambling *possessed* all of us, boy and man. Whether we consciously thought of it as a way out of the neighborhood or not I don't know. We certainly knew of its dangers, witness the beating that made such a lasting impression on the entire neighborhood. If we got out of high school and became longshoremen, or maybe into the sanitation department, we still gambled. It was part of our lives; it clung to us like a sour smell.

How else can it be that at my age, so far removed from my childhood and my neighborhood, I still remember the name Volo Yates, and the day that that horse made the neighborhood well?

When I would come home to West Seventh Street at six o'clock on a warm summer evening, front doors would be open, and radios in living rooms would be turned on loud, so the people sitting on the porches could hear the race results coming in over the Italian radio station. As I walked down the street all I heard was the staccato delivery of Charlie Backner with the results. And all I smelled was meat sauce coming from the open front doors. Meat sauce and racing were what the neighborhood was all about.

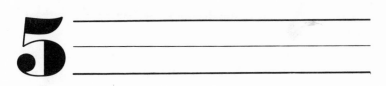

5

The worst horseplayer in the entire neighborhood was one of our neighborhood doctors, Dr. Ferdinand Gorgo, a man of about fifty who had a medical degree from the old country. He spoke Italian most of the time, but when pressed could use a bit of English.

Actually, Dr. Gorgo was one of about five Italian doctors in the neighborhood, but since he was the Della Femina doctor I know more about him. The rumor was that he had gone to medical school in the United States but had flunked out. He then supposedly got himself admitted to the medical school in Bologna, where he went on to become a doctor. He then came back to the United States to practice. He was an incredibly incompetent physician, but doctors didn't make it in our neighborhood by spectacular diagnosis; they developed a reputation with the old ladies. If the grandmothers liked a doctor's style and bedside manner, his name was passed from old lady to old lady and his practice was built upon this foundation.

Gorgo was grossly overweight, he smoked too much, and he didn't take care of himself at all. The reason he didn't take care of himself was that he was addicted to the horses and this addiction fit right into the neighborhood. He spent more time with the horses than he did with humans and my uncle said he should have been a veterinarian. Many a bookie paid a visit to the doctor in perfect health, and left even healthier.

Gorgo's affliction was well known throughout the neighborhood because a secret like horseplaying was really not a secret at all. He lived in two rooms behind a tiny office; he reportedly was married, but no one ever saw his wife, and he had no children. His office/residence was on West Twelfth Street and Avenue U, right in the middle of the neighborhood.

Gorgo's method of treating a patient was the same whether the person had a wart or walking pneumonia, catarrh or cancer: he first tried to scare the daylights out of him. A patient would walk into his office and the first words out of Gorgo's mouth were, "My God, how did you ever let yourself get into this condition?" Even if his patient were twelve or thirteen, Gorgo had visions of death. "You shouldn't allow this to happen," he would say. "Do you know what you have? Do you have any idea of what is wrong with you?" By this time the poor patient would be hysterical, backed against the wall, and ready to move next door to George's Funeral Home, where Gorgo buried his mistakes.

The harangue was always conducted in Italian, and

Gorgo usually would be building up to tell someone that he had the flu.

One day Gorgo paid a house call on a man named Salvatore, who had been complaining of chest pains. Salvatore lived only two blocks away from Gorgo's office. In Gorgo walked, tried to take Salvatore's pulse, thumped his chest once or twice, and pronounced him in perfect shape. The chest pains were badly cooked sausage. Gorgo walked out of the house and the next day Salvatore dropped dead of a heart attack.

My grandmother was a patient of Gorgo's because he reassured her, and when Salvatore dropped dead my grandmother chalked it up to poor information given to the doctor by the patient, not poor doctoring. And yet, when I think of Gorgo and his patients, I have to admit that his patients — at least the old ladies — lived to the age of seventy (anybody dying before seventy died prematurely) and mostly they lived to their eighties and nineties.

But how could any patient seriously believe in a doctor whose hours didn't start until 3:45, which was the time he usually got back from the track? He wasn't affiliated with any hospital, and he never referred a patient to a specialist. No one in the neighborhood ever had brain surgery. Gorgo didn't know about brain surgery.

Although "Do you know what you have?" was his primary statement to patients, he also had a habit of coming into the house, taking a quick run upstairs to look at the sick individual, and then saying to the family assembled downstairs, "Well, she's very sick." If that didn't make the patient's family hysterical, nothing did.

Occasionally, he would recommend sending a very sick

patient to either Coney Island Hospital or the Kings Highway Hospital. However, none of his patients wanted to go to either hospital, because the hospitals were in alien territory and, to tell the truth, he never pushed or made an issue of it. Gorgo seemed to know that most of his patients could not be helped by hospitals and probably would have been made even sicker.

Nobody was ever specifically told by the doctor what he or she was sick from. Gorgo was not very strong on giving out details. Just, "He's very sick." And to most families that was enough. People in the neighborhood simply got sick and then died. They either died immediately after getting sick (like one or two days) or they lingered for months. But once a patient got sick, that was that. They really didn't recover.

Cancer never was a problem in the neighborhood. Nobody knew what the hell it was. Or heart disease. My grandfather got sick in 1947. Gorgo rushed in, told all of us gathered in the living room that grandfather was very sick, that we ought to get him to a hospital, but that if grandfather refused the hospital, he, Gorgo, would of course continue house calls, as was his wont. My grandfather went to the hospital and died the next day. We never knew why; and certainly the doctor didn't know.

My cousin Eddy's bad cough might have been lung cancer, but neither we nor Gorgo ever knew; one day Eddy up and died. The patient would be very sick; the next day, death. And the neighborhood, right down to the last hypochondriac, simply would say, "Well, he's gone, but what a good life he had."

One of my relatives was a lush. In a neighborhood of boozers, this guy was really head and shoulders over everyone else. His was a classic case of cirrhosis and his liver had turned to sawdust, and no one — certainly not his doctor — had the sense to say, "Cut out the drinking and you'll live another twenty years or so." He kept drinking wine and kept getting a stronger shade of yellow as the days wore on. One day his liver gave out; in fact, his entire body quit. So he died, at the age of seventy.

Gorgo did turn out to be very quick in learning about penicillin. When that drug was just reaching the market, he decided that this was the drug for him to work with. So everyone got penicillin, no matter what the undiagnosed disease was, no matter if the patient might be allergic to the drug. Down with the pants and *zonk!* — another hit of the miracle drug. I am convinced that he tried to cure cancer with penicillin. If my mother's great-uncle was bright yellow and tired and complaining of aches and pains, it wasn't hepatitis, it was just the need for a quick shot of penicillin.

Sometimes his diagnosis was so far off that he even failed to prescribe penicillin when it might have helped. When my grandmother was dying at the age of eighty-four, with hardening of the arteries, a chronic case of pneumonia, and a lung condition, Gorgo missed the diagnosis and didn't give the penicillin. But he was smart enough to say to all of us, "You can keep her at home. You can keep her." Thus, he did not develop the reputation of "hospital doctor," the kind of quack who sent his patients off to the hospital to die. Unfortunately, in my grandmother's case he even misread her vital signs and the fact that they were quickly ebbing. "She's very bad, but I'll be back," he said, on one of his daily visits. Boy, he wasn't kidding. He went out the door and down the block and my grandmother muttered some Italian prayer and died. Just like that. One of us went running out the door to try and catch Gorgo, did, and brought him back. The doctor simply looked at my grandmother and kept saying, "I told you she was very bad. I told you so."

Because my father had a steady job we kids in the family had a different doctor — Dr. Sherman — who wasn't a pediatrician, nor was he a specialist. He simply was the doctor for the younger members of the family. Sherman was Jewish, which may be why he didn't catch on with the older people. He also couldn't hack the language.

And then one day a young Italian showed up right off the boat. His name was Guido — Dr. Guido — and he was a very good-looking guy and very smooth. He started to give Gorgo real competition. His gimmick was that he had just gotten out of medical school — I think in Rome — and his accent was heavy beyond belief. Not only did the old ladies become entranced with him, but his dark complexion did a job on the fiftyish daughters of the old ladies.

He's in the neighborhood today, and still doing quite nicely with the older people. How he managed to pick our neighborhood is still a mystery. Maybe the Italian medical schools have some kind of placement bureau that puts out a report saying there's a neighborhood in Brooklyn, U.S.A., with very few doctors, including one who's addicted to horses. And thus we got Dr. Guido.

The interesting thing about Guido is that he was much younger than Gorgo, but he knew all of the old tricks. He was especially good at painting throats with argyrol, which is a foul-tasting black stuff the neighborhood relied on to cure every disease located in the throat. Neither Gorgo nor Guido ever said, "Gee, you're running a temperature of a hundred and three and you've got a red throat, maybe I ought to take a culture just to make sure you don't have anything real serious." Never. They'd reach for the black argyrol, swab the offending throat, get the arm out of the way quickly so the patient didn't throw up on them, and send the patient home.

The only time the practice of medicine ever got out of the local doctors' hands occurred back in 1947, when we had a smallpox scare. The schools put a lot of pressure on the parents to have their children vaccinated, and there were long lines of kids at Coney Island Hospital.

One of the tragedies of all the neighborhood doctors was they simply did not know about corrective medicine, restorative medicine, surgery to *fix* people who desperately needed fixing. My neighborhood doesn't have many pretty people. There are people with harelips, and clubbed feet, and crossed eyes, and horrendous skin conditions, and teeth that desperately need fixing. The neighborhood did not know about making people more *average*-looking. We were unaware that medicine *was* making progress in other parts of the world.

God knows how many kids went without glasses because their parents would say, "I don't want my kid being a four-eyes." What these parents were really saying was they didn't want to go outside the neighborhood and deal with the intricacies of getting glasses prescribed for their children. In fact, they didn't know about getting pupils dilated and eyes tested for glasses. The neighborhood did not believe in outsiders in any way, shape, or form, and that included eye specialists and hospitals. My father went to a hospital for treatment of an ulcer, but only because the company he worked for had a doctor on the premises who *insisted* he go to the hospital. None of the neighborhood longshoremen were told by a "company doctor" to go to the hospital for treatment.

I've often thought about the level of medical treatment in the neighborhood and I've finally come to the conclusion that it wasn't a matter of economics, but ignorance. If a girl was born and she was beautiful except for a hooked nose and some teeth that needed straightening, the nose stayed hooked and the teeth remained crooked. If the girl's family had known that there was indeed plastic surgery to aid people physically (and psychologically) they would have found the money to get the surgery. But they had never heard of it. They were still living on the slopes of Mount Etna, and the word on plastic surgery hadn't reached Mount Etna.

If the physical but fixable blemishes were bad, the cases of retardation in the neighborhood were worse. The reversion to Old Country attitude was just about complete if a child was mongoloid or retarded. There was only one thing to do: hide the offending offspring. There were about eight or nine retarded children in our neighborhood, and their lives were hell. Not only did they have their own disability to cope with, but they also were the subject of ridicule and scorn. The mongoloids were all herded into a special class in P.S. 95. The families of such children only knew how to be mortally embarrassed. They didn't know about possible institutionalizing, or how to seek trained help.

The proprietors of one of the candy stores in the neighborhood had a retarded child named Jimmy, and all his parents could do was build him a wooden wagon, which was a substitute for a wheelchair.

The big fear among diseases was polio. The rest of the world was avoiding close contact in the summertime, staying out of swimming pools, avoiding overexertion. Avenue U in Brooklyn took another course: every kid in the neighborhood wore a small packet of raw camphor around his or her neck. Hundreds of packets of camphor mysteriously appeared during the polio epidemics and every child wore one.

This wasn't the turn of the century. This was the United States in 1949. We had fought a war; we had gone through sulfa and were into the next generation of miracle drugs; Sister Kenny and the March of Dimes were doing their number. But the old ladies of Brooklyn were sticking to their camphor bags. Forget that they hadn't been in Sicily for forty years. Sicily still clung to them like olive oil.

If camphor is strange, the old ladies also had a hand in witchcraft. Let us say, hypothetically, that someone who wished my parents evil came into our home. And I was standing around. The guest, with evil in his or her heart, might give me the "eye," or an "overlook." If I was "overlooked," a curse had been put on me and then, naturally, my parents had to exorcise it. We didn't put in a call for an exorcist; practically any old lady over the age of seventy with a dark dress was able to put together a little ceremony to get rid of the evil eye. The tipoff to whether a person had been "overlooked" or not depended upon what the evil person said. Signal phrases such as "What a *lovely* child you have" from a particularly evil person meant that the overlook had to be removed and plenty fast.

If a kid was overlooked and his parents happened not to be around, the child was sometimes aware of the evil eye because of a headache. "I got a headache," was enough warning to gather the old ladies — three or four of them — for a quick ceremony.

The crucial part of getting rid of the overlook consisted of dropping a pair of scissors on the floor. What the hell it signified I'm not sure, but I assume it had something to do with cutting out the evil eye. After the scissors were dropped a little packet of garlic was hung around the kid's neck (making sure it did not get in the way of the camphor) and a touch of olive oil (on the forehead) was added to the mixture. My wife remembers how an evil eye had been hung on someone in her family and every night they went through the ritual of getting out the garlic, oil, and scissors.

If we were short-handed when it came to doctors, the situation with dentists was much worse. There were two dentists: one Jewish, who mistakenly moved into the neighborhood; the other an Italian who had attended an Italian dental school.

The Italian dentist didn't do much of a business either. We were a society who began the day brushing with salt (which might be okay) but we sure as hell knew nothing whatsoever about dental care. The Italian, Dr. Bellitti, didn't encourage dental sophistication among his patients. His offices were under the Culver Line Elevated. The noise from the train was such that Bellitti never knew when he was drilling or not. He was perfectly suited to the neighborhood. He was skilled enough to do extractions and, on rare occasions, a filling or two. But that was it. The people in the neighborhood really didn't believe in filling cavities; their secret was to let the tooth rot away until Bellitti came in to pull the stump.

A gummy smile was a status symbol. There's a very old man living on my block with one lonely stub in his mouth;

that remaining tooth is a mark of distinction. Bellitti didn't do much in the way of business, and Snyder, the other dentist, did absolutely nothing.

We had no lawyers who lived in the neighborhood. Nor, for that matter, *any* professional men. What we did have was a guy named Gambetta who was quite similar to the character Calhoun on the old "Amos 'n' Andy" series. Gambetta had a store, where he operated as a combination real estate broker, semi–legal adviser, notary public, and preparer of income tax forms. "Forms" is the key here; Gambetta could read and write English, which was an accomplishment. He helped the neighborhood cope with the outside world.

When real trouble arrived in the neighborhood, the residents reluctantly sought Jewish advice, something which they wouldn't have done — because of their anti-Semitic feelings — unless they were up against the wall. If the family finally realized that someone was dreadfully ill, there was a Jewish doctor on call, but everyone had to agree to his being called in. If a kid got into very heavy criminal trouble — really bad — the lawyer produced by the family invariably was Jewish. Mr. Kahn was our landlord. He owned our house and fifteen other houses in the neighborhood. He was an outside force, and feared.

Our neighborhood did not produce friendly doctors like the one in *The Last Angry Man,* who returned to practice medicine in the area for decades after getting out of medical school. Nor did we produce friendly (but neighborhood) cops who came back home to walk a beat and provide affectionate (but firm) guidance to the kids growing up. That was a vision reserved for Irish cop movies.

Occasionally, cops would drive into the neighborhood

and make a few stops. During the stops the affectionate (but firm) neighborhood bookie would stick his head into the window of the police car and — who knows? maybe they were discussing the weather.

Yes, we did have one beat cop — an ancient Italian who somehow wangled his way onto the force. Our cop, Rugantino, turned out to be the totally corrupt policeman, even though he could barely speak English. Rugantino was eventually thrown off the force when it was discovered that he was working out the details for robberies with three kids from the area and taking a piece of the action.

The reason we had no homegrown doctors or dentists or lawyers was quite simple: the neighborhood did not go to work wearing a suit. Everyone wore real blue collars. We had no suits. We were car mechanics, bus mechanics, truck mechanics. We were into lifting things, picking up boxes from one pile and moving them four feet to another pile. We were expert at unloading ships, trains, and trucks. If we didn't shape up on the Brooklyn docks at 5 A.M., we were arriving at our jobs by 6. We rarely left Brooklyn, but if we did it was to go to work as fishmongers in the Fulton Fish Market in Lower Manhattan. We also were heavy on working in printing shops.

We were the people who made things go, move, get done. You might say we were the American equivalent of Sicilian peasants, except that our peasantry was tied to a mechanical society. If we weren't making things move or shifting heavy objects from one stack to another, we were behind the counter, in our own neighborhood, slicing meat or cutting cheese. Our neighborhood were strong union people; we believed in unions and they were the only organized *thing* we belonged to.

Our aspirations were nonexistent. There weren't real doctors in the area to encourage a kid to push and go into medicine. There wasn't a real lawyer around to be truly helpful. So the man next door was a tailor who worked for Barney's; the guy across the street was a garage mechanic. Down a few houses from the mechanic was a milkman and across the street from him was an elevator operator. The grandmothers were saying, "Nobody home," and our mothers and fathers were saying, "Go to trade school." I suppose the fathers were correct in pushing trade schools so their children wouldn't have to fix, push, carry, lift, and move. Their vision could only see beyond their current bad back. There always was a boss.

It wasn't that the great American dream eluded the neighborhood or passed it by. It simply never existed.

I'd walk into a house and see a pile of cloth on a dining room table, and I knew even then that I wasn't looking at hot goods but piece goods. The woman of the house did edging by hand to earn a little extra money. My mother did edging. My father came home from the *Times* at six at night, grabbed supper, and in the summertime went over to Coney Island to his second job, where he supervised one of the rides until two in the morning. He hated the job — but we needed the money.

If there were piece goods in the house, then the boss was undoubtedly Jewish. Somewhere along the line sociologists got the notion that Italians and Jews, both family-structured societies, were quite similar in ethnic makeup and got along with one another more readily than, say, did Italians and Irish. No truth to that. The Italians did not like the Jews.

Forget about the Mafia and all of its hocus-pocus.

Italians generally are *secretive* and never show the world what they're really thinking. Somehow, Italians fostered the notion that they were fun-loving, perpetually singing, pasta-stuffing, laughing folks. Utter nonsense, but an illusion skillfully put out by the Italians to confuse the opposition. Someone who is Jewish may go into an Italian's home, eat his pasta, and laugh it up all evening, but when he leaves the Italian will talk behind his back. As a matter of fact, the Italian will talk behind any non-Italian's back. Code words, arcane dialects, secretive communication between blood brothers sworn to *omertà* even though they're law-abiding citizens.

Nobody told us about the chances of our being able to wear a white shirt and tie to work, so all of us kids went out and got jobs pushing, moving, lifting, delivering *little* kid-sized things. I became a messenger delivering advertising proofs. I was eighteen at the time and in delivering proofs to Lord & Taylor, Saks, and Bonwit, I happened to glimpse that there was another world beyond Avenue U. My friends were not so lucky. They didn't have fathers who could get their kids jobs as messengers in *Manhattan.* One friend got a job as a minor clerk (if you can believe that!) in a grocery store and he's still working in that grocery store to this day. No, he doesn't now own it; he just works there.

The kids entered the system and their first jobs were very often a preview of what they had in store for the rest of their lives. I never heard a friend say, "Gee, I think I'm going to found the Sicilian Asphalt and Paving Company." It wasn't in the programmed scheme of things.

Fathers and sons would get home at 6:30 at night, exhausted. They'd eat their dinners and probably drink too much wine. If they had any strength left, they'd tend to things around their own homes which needed lifting, moving, fixing, etc. All of us were extremely good at fixing cars, and on a quiet summer night you could look down the blocks and see dozens of kids deep into the bowels of their cars. During the winter, we painted our houses and added on extra rooms. Nobody ever said, "Well, here's our new room, I guess we better get the roofer in here." If the roof had to be tarred, we tarred it ourselves. We broke down walls, plumbed, wired, and did the whole thing.

The women talked about food and the men talked about baseball. No one ever sat down and complained about his or her lot. They assumed the entire world lived as they did. In many respects, they were satisfied. They brought home a paycheck; people in the family were fed and housed and what more was there to life? Most of the residents in the neighborhood were nervous in any kind of social or occupational situation that was different from their worker-bee situation. No one wanted to be in charge of a ten-man work force. Too much responsibility. And, as one uncle once said to me, "What the hell do I need that for? I'll have to wear a tie." He couldn't handle it. It was way beyond him. My uncle was expressing a neighborhood belief that the tie was a symbol of authority. The grandfather to the father to the child: beware of the man wearing a tie, he's going to try and pull one over on you.

Unlike other vast immigrations to this country, of men who wanted to better themselves, the Italians just wanted to get the hell out of a condition which was infinitely worse. They came to be together, as I said earlier. And by God, when Christmas rolled around and they were together, that's all that counted. Forget no money, no security, crooked teeth, crooked eyes, no education. That's bullshit.

Now it is true that one part of the neighborhood went outside Avenue U and robbed the hell out of liquor stores, and grocery stores. But even then the robbers weren't truly trying to better their existence: they wanted to live like the rest of us without doing any of the labor. No real ambition. No Cary Grant struggling as a cat burglar to pay for the villa on the French Riviera.

I never heard any introspective talk from my family about what it was like "back there." Nor did I get any travelogues from any of my relatives who came over. My mother and all of my friends' parents had been "back there." They had "left back there" because it was lousy. They "came here." Why should they complain about old Dr. Gorgo? He was as much from "back there" as he was from here.

We were a Neapolitan tribe, secretive, uncomplaining, telling each other not to make waves. Don't shoot for anything too much. The only entrepreneurial push in the entire neighborhood came from the funeral home guys, and they coined money. God knows how or why anyone aspired to owning a funeral home, but they did.

Our heroes were very true to the character of the neighborhood. We didn't really look up to a politician like Fiorello LaGuardia; besides, he wasn't Italian all the way through. In the 1940s we looked up to sport figures — DiMaggio, the boxer Willie Pep, Yogi Berra.

We were a closed society, and it stemmed all the way back to the grandparents. My grandmother could not handle the alien card at the post office. We didn't go out to restaurants because we thought we'd be made fun of. Maybe we wouldn't be able to read the menu and the waiter would laugh at us. So we'll stay home. We'll stay in our neighbor-hood and we'll work together and we'll stick to speaking Italian. And the people in the neighborhood were walking around saying we'll hate the Jews because they're outside the area and they seem to be coping with life; they're doing better than we are.

But, above all else, we'll not venture into any profession whatsoever that requires any risk. Don't push, don't strive. In other words, live through life with dirty fingernails. The bottom line on Avenue U: it was a neighborhood of grease under the nails — honestly put there, but destined always to remain.

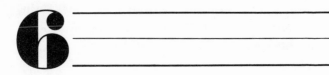

6

Professional achievement means education. I wish I were able to say that the saving grace in growing up in Gravesend was the schools, but they weren't. It would sound ethnically and properly American to say that the schools helped us to survive. For me, and the rest of my friends, school had nothing to do with education but everything to do with occupying young people's *time* until they were ready to join their parents in lifting, pushing, pulling, and stacking.

The grammar schools were used to try to assimilate the neighborhood into the United States of America. I spoke not a word of English when I started school at the age of six. But then why should I have? Italian was spoken at home. I lived in a claustrophobically Italian neighborhood; everyone I knew spoke only Italian, so it was quite natural that

I didn't know English. The grammar schools also tried to teach the barbarians among us why we should have small-pox shots, what a bank account was, and other simple standards of life. Junior high school was quite different: it provided the educational backdrop for sex and gambling and crime. All of the neighborhood gangsters began to test their wings in junior high school. High school was the last stop. It simply was a holding action, either as a trade school — mechanics, printing — or until the student was old enough to leave without a parent's permission.

There sure as hell weren't any Mr. Chipses or Miss Doves in either P.S. 95, P.S. 228, or Lafayette High School. Or at least I didn't spot them. There seemed to be a loose combination of forces in the neighborhood made up of the Church, the Mafia, the Board of Education, all of which were aligned in a strange way. What "they" did was very clever: they built a decent, respectable-looking neighborhood. Physically the neighborhood could be set down into any working-class section of the United States. But the ghetto mentality was built in psychologically and mentally.

Why is it, for example, that every kid whom I knew attending P.S. 95 failed to go to college? Why did the neighborhood schools turn out a succession of guys who today, at the age of forty-five, still only know how to stand in front of a candy store and shoot dice?

I think the answer is that they only knew the American nightmare, not the American dream. Although the Mafia certainly knew and nurtured our neighborhood, the Establishment that ran the Church and the Board of Education did not know about us. They crossed us off their maps early on. No one at the very top of either organization ever said, "Let's try to do something for the Gravesend section of Brooklyn." At 110 Livingston Street, which is the headquarters of the Board of Education, they simply said in effect, "Forget this district. They're going to be bums no matter what we do, so let's not spend the money or the personnel and try to salvage them." As for the Church, they only saw us as potential revenue, and putting some of that money back into the neighborhood was not in their scheme of things.

The word "college" was never mentioned in junior high school or high school. That word was from a foreign language. No teacher, or guidance counsellor, or principal ever said, "Improve your life! Go out and continue your education!" The teachers weren't interested in the school, the principals weren't interested in the school, and the parents were worried about too much reading.

I think that some of the teachers originally might have wanted to teach something. But I also believe that when they saw the conditions that they would have to work under, they didn't know what to do. They started out to be teachers and they wound up as keepers.

Most of our teachers were Irish. So they were our first keepers, along with the Irish cops.

We didn't hate our Irish teachers. Yes, we would say "those fucking Irish teachers," but it didn't have the strength that the anti-Semitism did in the neighborhood. Mrs. O'Connor, Mrs. O'Reilly, and Mrs. Stafford were the crazy ladies who would sit in front of the class, and if a kid didn't toe the mark they'd simply pick up the kid and slam him against the wall. I'd just be sitting there and suddenly find myself being beaten against the wall. We had one

Italian teacher out of the entire mob, Mrs. De Buono, and she acted the same way the Irish teachers did: never a word about climbing out of the mess we lived in but a swift shot for anyone who fooled around.

There is another side to the argument. There were thirty kids in a grammar school class, all of whom had very little interest in education. Additionally, there would be five borderline psychotics who had the tough-kid syndrome, and had to prove to the class that they were potential members of the Mafia. We had the problem of macho in those days, but we didn't have a name for it.

Mrs. Cole was my first-grade teacher and she was sympathetic but not very helpful. She was stuck with a class of kids who couldn't speak English, and sometimes she would get confused as to whether the kid was having problems understanding *anything* or simply English. She never took it upon herself to call home and find out if the kid was retarded, or Italian, or both.

Kids of all capabilities were lumped together. Potential killers with I.Q.'s of 85 and 90 were thrown in with others who could have learned something.

The parents weren't that interested in school either. They weren't sitting there saying, "Let's see what your school marks are." My parents never went to the school to discuss my progress with the teachers. Whenever a parent went to school it was to discuss the teacher's hitting the kid. The parent, in most cases, wanted to tell the teacher, "Hey, he's my kid, I'll rap him." With this, the kid would get a second shot.

If the teachers were taking random swings at kids, by the seventh grade the kids were slugging teachers. Kids would be fighting each other in class, teachers — men and women — were getting hit, and the scene was one of eternal bedlam.

We studied the usual things — arithmetic, geography, English — but we didn't study them in the usual way. One day we were trying to get through a little ancient history, Sparta and Athens. One of the kids was reading aloud to the class and in the middle of the recitation a junior thug named Paone started talking about how he led a gang and broke into a boat tied up in Sheepshead Bay. Although the gang got very little of value, the raid — by a bunch of seventh-graders — was the current talk of the school.

The teacher said, "Quiet, Paone!" Paone said calmly, "Go fuck yourself." At this point the teacher threatened Paone with a pink card, which was the disciplinary stigma at school. Students had to take their cards to the principal's office and find out what their punishment was going to be.

The threat of a pink card didn't stop Paone for a moment. And the class had to decide whether to listen to the teacher trying to talk about Athens or listen to Paone. Obviously, Paone was more interesting because he was a lot closer to the neighborhood and anyhow, who cared about Athens or Sparta? Paone was young and glamorous, Sparta was old and dull. From the seventh grade on everyone knew he was going to be something in the Mob; he was going to make the big time. The seventh grade was not that far off the mark about Paone. He did make the Mob and ended up running a funeral home in the neighborhood. But something went wrong and he got terribly beaten up and almost died.

We were adults at an early age. We cut classes and would shoot craps at the pizza store or the candy store. The teachers simply wanted to get through the day and then leave the neighborhood and go back home. There were no teachers from my neighborhood. They all came from the outside, traveling to and from and not understanding at all the children they were supposed to be teaching.

One of the problems was that we were a neighborhood of gamblers and the only thing we knew well was percentages. "What's the odds of staying in school anyhow?" one of my friends named Rick once said to me. And that about summed up education on Avenue U. My friends found it easier to prepare to leave school early than to prepare for education. In the eighth and ninth grades, they began to cut classes. The number of kids leaving Lafayette High School before graduation was phenomenal. The Jewish students — to a man — stayed in school.

The situation in the parochial school was not much different. Even though the Church schools had God on their side, education was a loser. In those schools the teachers — lay and priest — were devoted to the talent hunt. Where are the future nuns and priests? The teachers were pushing monastery and nunnery, and if the student they spotted as having potential had little interest in a Church career, forget it — train him to be a messenger.

I found out that it was easier to make a wisecrack than study; it was simpler to fool around. My fellow-students appreciated me more when I didn't study, which is why I was a poor student. The high point of my school life took place when the principal called my mother up and told her that my conduct had been improving.

I had the potential for learning. Although I never did learn how to spell, reading stuck and not only was my reading fast, but my comprehension levels were high. In the tenth grade we participated in a citywide reading test.

I finished the test quickly, walked up to the teacher, and handed her the test. "Get back to your seat, you can't be finished," she said. I sat down and five minutes later I went up to the teacher and tried to give her the test. This time I got yelled at: "This is a citywide test and you're disrupting." Finally, ten minutes later, she accepted my test. It turned out that I ran second in the city; a kid from Columbus High School was first.

My teachers were shocked at the reading score and became very paranoid. They figured it was a hell of a mistake. After all, they said, he can't spell, he's a terrible fuck-up in class, therefore why should he be able to read?

As for the rest of the guys in the class, they looked at me the way they looked at the Jewish students, all of whom were getting immense pressure from home to get ready for college and the world. The Italian students never got this kind of message at home. The Italians, well, they too were getting a picture of what life was going to be like for them but it had nothing to do with education.

The schools wrecked thousands of lives. A friend of mine named Bobby is forty-six and has never moved out of the neighborhood. He was a printer and now he's been phased out of work. He called me the other day in desperation, saying he couldn't find a job of any kind and didn't know how he was going to feed his family. Bobby is a bright guy and he's begging to be a messenger. What really frightened me was hearing Bobby say, "When I go to places looking for work they're looking for younger people."

Forty-six and terribly bitter, and capable of being much better in life. The neighborhood and the system killed him but they didn't have the courtesy to bury him. They simply sent him out into the world. Peter, another friend of mine, wanted to become a lawyer but the neighborhood, which taught him to fear trying to be somebody or something different, made him look for a "safe" position. He's been a low-paid civil servant and the frustration has given him bleeding ulcers.

I look back on the whole educational process and it's as if someone set aside a section of Brooklyn and started to train the messengers of the future. Do you know what it's like to visit your neighborhood and see the wreckage left behind? One close friend named Al was raised to become a waiter for the rest of his life. Another guy, Frank, hustles cheap watches in a neighborhood jewelry store. Nicolo and another friend named Ronnie both became printers. Tulio and Charlie, fifty-year-old commission salesmen. Bob ended up driving an oil truck; another fellow named Sal is a tailor. A friend named Paul simply dropped out of sight; for all I know, he's dead. One guy ended up owning his own pizza stand: he's the local success story — we point to him with pride. He's a success compared to Al, who is still cutting meat. Al is cutting meat for someone else.

I sometimes wake up in the middle of the night in a stone-cold sweat saying, "Jesus, what a close call. They almost got me." My friends from West Seventh Street are faced with a lifetime of paranoia. They ride the trains, fight the crowds, struggle, and feel that the world is against them. They are right: the world is against them.

The only real outlet for the neighborhood was sports, and we went at them with wild enthusiasm. Although we absorbed nothing inside the schools, the schoolyards were a fantastic part of our education. Schoolyards were handy:

we used them as a place for sports, as a place for sex, for gambling, for any kind of endeavor.

The P.S. 95 schoolyard was concrete, surrounded by a fence, with a lot of nooks and crannies where we could hide from the outside world. I would show up after three o'clock and start playing ball, but on Sundays we always would gather in one of the corners and run a crap game. If we got into a fight, it was settled in the schoolyard. We'd play ball in the afternoon, and be back in the schoolyard at night with a girl.

The P.S. 95 schoolyard was off Avenue U, between Lake and Van Sicklen streets. There were two candy stores right across the street. Although P.S. 95 officially "educated" children from the first through the sixth grades, everyone up to the age of twenty-five (and sometimes older) "hung around."

At three, when school let out, the small kids went home and athletics began in earnest. Softball was played from three until dark, and on any Saturday the "big" game would begin at nine o'clock in the morning, promptly, and run till nine at night. The softball game was on one side of the schoolyard and the half-court basketball games were on the other side. There was enough room for both games, although the left fielder occasionally found himself setting a pick for a basketball player driving for the basket.

Until three, the rest of the kids in the neighborhood were either in junior high school (David H. Boody Junior High), or working on their fathers' fruit trucks, or shaping up as longshoremen. At three, they headed for P.S. 95's schoolyard.

We behaved in that schoolyard. Despite the influx of outside (and older) children, that school was never vandalized, never ripped off. It was left untouched. We left the place alone because schools were threatening enough when you belonged there. Nobody wanted to get into a school, whether for vandalism or for study. I cannot recall even one incident of attempted vandalism. If a window broke, a ball hit it, and when that happened, we were all a little nervous because we didn't want to lose this precious bit of territory that was ours.

Once, a janitor had taken to locking up the schoolyard doors on both sides with a huge lock. Some guys in the neighborhood simply hacked off the locks with a huge ax, which was provided by a local bar to some of the older guys. A forty-year-old guy named Harry, who hadn't seen the schoolyard in twenty-five years, knocked off the lock and the crowd from the bar cheered him, almost like a ship launching. It was the neighborhood's way of telling the Board of Education, "Don't screw around with our school-yard — it's ours; it belongs to us."

On a nice spring Saturday fifty guys would be using the schoolyard. Eighteen kids might be playing softball. Another six kids playing basketball, and another three hanging around to play the winners. Add to that a number of people waiting to get into the softball game. There were always spectators, and in the areas not taken over by sports, there would be card games. The crap games never really started until Sunday. We also played a one-man game called fast pitching, which consisted of a kid throwing his arm out against a strike zone drawn on a wall. All the game took was a Spalding and imagination. One kid named Frank would provide a complete play-by-play (drawn from real life) as he pitched: "Branca waits while Thompson digs in, he gets his sign, and the first pitch in to Thompson is low and outside, ball one." On Frank went, and if the spectators couldn't afford the price of a radio to listen to the real games, Frank was able to give them the next best thing.

Gravesend — indeed, Brooklyn — produced more than its share of potential big-league ball players. It was a way out of the neighborhood. But just about every player carried with him the seeds of destruction, also provided by the neighborhood. Take, for example, a ball player I'll call Billy Carlos. He was typical neighborhood in that he always wanted to take the easy way out, and if somebody bothered him, Billy would think nothing of punching rather than talking. He had a wise-guy attitude.

Billy was signed by the Chicago White Sox after a fantastic career as a ball player in high school. Wow, we thought. Neighborhood kid with big league contract! Billy was sent down to the minors, and in those days the minor leagues were big organizations. He had a good first year, struck out a lot of guys, hit about .325, and got into a lot of trouble. He started to act like a wise-ass and he never made it to Chicago. He got back to the neighborhood and today he works at an uncle's fruit and vegetable stand. He still has his temper and he still is a wise guy and he could have made the big leagues if he hadn't carried his neighborhood attitude with him.

Another player was a fellow named Willie Marcantonio, who also had the same fantastic potential, also was right up there in the minors, hitting about .340, and also had the same neighborhood problem of hitting first and asking questions later. He swung at every manager he ever played for and finally he was told to quit the game: he would never make it because of his temper. Willie moved to Queens a long time ago, but I still hear about him. He has a small shoe-repair shop. He always had good hands and he picked up fixing shoes from his grandfather, and that's how he's been supporting himself all these years. He never married, he boozes with the rest of the neighborhood guys every Saturday night, and of course he's heavy into gambling. In truth, he's a beautiful person, but his violent temper was the problem. Temper, however, was the neighborhood, not just Willie. He, and all of us, had violence coded into us. He couldn't shake the neighborhood: wherever he went, the streets were following close behind.

When the minor-league team Willie had been playing for finally sent him back to Brooklyn for the last time, Willie was received as a conquering hero. One day Willie was gleefully telling some of us about the time one of his managers told him to take a hundred laps around the ball field and Willie simply told the manager to go fuck himself. There went the career.

Obviously I can only speculate, but our neighborhood paid homage to ball players the way Harlem treated boxers. Not that our Willie Marcantonio was a Sugar Ray Robinson, but we literally sat at Willie's knee. We *all* wanted to become ball players.

On quiet summer nights we sat arguing the merits of a Rizzuto, Reiser, Reese. Was it Snyder, or Mantle, or Mays? We filled our heads with what all kids lived for, stats: Nick Etton hit twenty-two home runs in 1945, but Snuffy Sternweiss led the American League in 1946 by hitting .309. Tony Cuccinello was second with .306 . . .

We were strictly baseball. Pro football was a schmuck sport and the only player anyone ever talked about was Bruiser Cunard, and that was because we liked his first name. Nobody cared about Army-Navy, and the only Old Alma Mater anyone was rooting for was Sicily. It's not quite accurate to say there wasn't any communication between father and son. But the only time fathers and sons did have anything to say to each other was about baseball: "You got your Mays, he's a credit to his race. You got your Tookey Gilbert, you got your . . . " The unifying factor in the household was the radio; turn it on, and both father and son listened.

We didn't know who the hell Truman was. But we all knew fielders like DiMaggio. Try to visualize what an entire neighborhood looked like, gracefully — that was the key word — gracefully ambling back to catch a fly ball to deep center and realizing, too late, that we were overly graceful and the ball was another forty feet over our heads? Forget about DiMaggio's contribution to the sport. Realize that he ruined an entire generation of kids who were desperately trying to amble back nonchalantly and catch deep flies to center.

Stan Musial affected us differently: we all screwed up our batting stance and looked like pretzels. Musial did it, why not us? Reiser spent a year or so recovering from concussions received from crashing into concrete walls, why shouldn't we give it the old Dodger try? Some of us perfected a wonderful combination of DiMaggio *and* Reiser, where we'd lope back gracefully and *then* crash into a wall.

Although softball was played in the schoolyard, hardball was played in something called Mark Twain Field over in Coney Island. If I didn't want to go out of the neighborhood to Coney Island, a hardball field had been carved out of one of the nearby dumps. Gravesend was surrounded by continually burning dumps, but some kids had managed to squeeze out a bit of room to make a hard-ball field. I couldn't drift back too casually on that field because I was liable to wind up in a bed of orange peels.

Joe Pepitone came out of our neighborhood and made it to the major leagues, but not without difficulty. When he was a student in Manual Trades High School another kid pointed a homemade zip gun at Pepitone and shot him in the stomach, almost killing him. Even Pepitone, who seemingly adapted enough to make it up to the majors, didn't have it very easy. He had trouble with behavior, trouble with managers, trouble with the outside world. Like all of those before him, he had trouble shaking the neighborhood he was desperately trying to leave behind him. Sandy Koufax came from Bay Parkway, which is the Jewish side of the neighborhood, and he went to the same high school as I did, Lafayette, at the same time. But Koufax was different; he was Jewish, and therefore automatically assumed to be more sensible about behavior than the Italians.

It wasn't that the kids who had the baseball talent were crazy themselves. They simply couldn't (or didn't know how to) function within an organization, and that means baseball or business. They had grown up seeing their fathers being told what to do and they must have resented it.

When we couldn't get into the softball game at the schoolyard and didn't feel like being graceful playing hardball among the garbage, we turned to stickball, just as in all New York neighborhoods. We had a crippled kid who pitched for both sides (with his crutch under one arm, pitching with the other), and we moved fairly languidly in the middle of traffic, too. Even in stickball, the DiMaggio influence persisted. If we read somewhere that DiMaggio spread his legs twenty-eight inches apart when he assumed his batting stance, then we spread our legs twenty-eight inches as well. None of us fourteen-year-old kids was more than fifty inches high, and I'll bet there's more than one early arthritic condition due to the DiMaggio stance.

Once in a while we got to the ball park, but not often. Partially, no money, but most of all out of the neighborhood — especially Yankee Stadium, which was a trip to a foreign country. To get to Ebbets Field, we had to take two trains. The Polo Grounds? It could just as well have been the moon. We *listened* — during the week, but especially on Sunday. We couldn't get through a Sunday meal without a game. The macaroni was served, and there's Red Barber.

We dreamed, we had visions, fantasies, and I suppose they were just like every other kid our age. One day the Saint Louis Cardinals were in town and some of them came to Coney Island to make a much-heralded personal appearance. I was about fourteen and Joe Garagiola, Tommy Glaviano, and Al Rice were the three Cardinals involved. The whole neighborhood showed up, but even then we were very cool. In the Midwest, I'm sure kids would have arrived with gloves and bats and autograph books. Not us. Sullen, skeptical, *very* cool, we just watched. There wasn't any loose talk about this guy's trading card, or that one's autograph. We didn't deal in such things; they couldn't be found in the neighborhood.

What impressed most of us was Glaviano, because he had suspenders on, underneath a business suit. In our neighborhood, the only men wearing suspenders were impoverished grandfathers right off the boat from Naples. Someone had set up a baseball-pitching machine and there were a few bats around. All of them took off their jackets, went into the batting cage, and took a few shots. None of the Cardinals was particularly good.

Although there was little antiblack feeling in the neighborhood, the only time the subject ever came up was with black ball players. Everyone conceded Jackie Robinson — he was once in a lifetime. The business of being black usually was discussed when a player like the Dodgers' pitcher Don Newcombe was mentioned. It was the consensus in the neighborhood that while a player like Newcombe might have his moments (like pitching ten perfect innings), in the end he'd fold under pressure (like letting Yogi Berra hit a home run off of him). Newcombe choked.

But there wasn't much generalized prejudice against the blacks when I was growing up. Blacks weren't around. Just a year ago, there was a nasty race riot at Lafayette High School. I can't even say that conditions were much better in the old days. They weren't. It has to be better in the schools today, despite the racial tensions, despite the overcrowding, the cutting back. The schools *can't* be worse than they used to be.

I don't live in the neighborhood, but I go back there and my family is still there. It's nothing but a time warp when I return. I look at the neighborhood and I see people who feel, despite what has or has not happened to them, that the system is still good. These are the same guys who don't know why we ever got out of Vietnam. "Should have leveled the entire fucking country and left it at that." The people I left behind stand up at Shea Stadium and sing "The Star Spangled Banner" — loud. These are the people who still go with the union, vote for the right thing, and believe in the American way of life. I never hear much said against the rotten school system. These are patriotic citizens, and if it was good enough for their fathers then it sure as hell is good enough for them.

I got a call the other day from a guy who had been a friend of mine and had a promising career ahead of him as a ball player but somehow screwed it up. Frankie, my friend, was out of a job again. "What happened to your last job?" I asked. "Oh," he said, "some Jew had it in for me and got me fired." I didn't say much, but I did ask him how things were in the neighborhood. "Pretty good," he said, "not bad at all." Things hadn't changed much, he said. I agreed with that.

I don't know where sex belonged when I was growing up, but it sure as hell didn't belong in the Italian home in my neighborhood.

If a woman got married under the proper circumstances and became pregnant later in the prescribed time, she was said to be in the "family way." Even the word "pregnant" was not used. And, no one — absolutely no one — ever went around smirking about how the woman got in the family way if her pregnancy was not within society's timetable.

This reticence about sex reflected the power structure of the community — who made the crucial decisions, who set the standards of behavior, who indeed *led* the community. In a word, the grandmothers. Although there were respected people within the community (store owners, funeral parlor proprietors, bookies), real respect was directly proportional to age: the older the better. The youngest member of any Italian family knew not to say much. At the dinner table, if the youngest was stupid enough to make a wisecrack the father or mother was always within hitting range. There was a silent generation in the community, the quite young. They didn't mouth off; if they had grievances they kept them to themselves. And they learned at an early age to treat the elderly with enormous respect.

The Roselli family lived down the street from us when I was growing up. I'm not sure of the exact order in which they arrived in this country, but I do know that they had an elderly grandmother still back in the old country, living in poverty in a tiny suburb of Naples. At a family council, all of them decided to bring the revered grandmother over to the United States. Donations were collected from uncles, aunts; all of them pitched in. Sure enough, Grandmother Roselli arrived one day and from the moment she stepped off the boat she became the leader of the family. Forget that she couldn't speak English, only a dialect of Italian which very few Italians outside of the neighborhood could comprehend.

Grandmother Roselli fit right in with the folks on West Seventh Street. The first thing she did was to lay her hands on a cheap deck chair, which she would drag out of the house every day from April through October and put outside on the sidewalk with the chairs of four or five other ladies. And then they would sit and talk, from dawn to dusk, settling things. I would walk down West Seventh Street during the summer and all I'd see on the sidewalks were clusters of chairs — four or five at the most — with four or five very old ladies apparently sitting around casually passing the time of day. Culture, mores, ethics, territorial rights — all the heavy stuff was decided by these ladies.

"Should Angelo have married Donna?"

"Why isn't Nicolo helping support his parents?"

And so on.

The leadership was a subtle thing: there wasn't any outward striving for it. When Grandmother Roselli moved in, the other ladies seemed to gravitate naturally toward her house. (In the winter, by the way, they would congregate in the leader's kitchen for endless cups of black coffee and continue the same conversations.)

Age was the overriding factor in leadership. We had an awful lot of dumb old ladies running things in the neighborhood, but by virtue of the fact that they had survived a plague or two in Italy, they were bright. Believe me, we didn't give any I.Q. tests to determine leadership qualities. When Grandmother Roselli arrived (and she must have been seventy-two or seventy-three when she got to this country), she immediately replaced several youngsters who were only in their late sixties.

As my own grandmother reached her late seventies, she grew a bit senile. But her senility was never mentioned by anyone; in fact, the older and more senile she got, the more questions she was asked and the more complicated problems she was begged — *begged* — to solve.

Opinions had nothing whatsoever to do with senility. Loss of bodily functions — well, that was a different situation. But as long as the tongue kept wagging, and the words kept coming out, the opinions were honored.

Our neighborhood did not know about, or accept, either senility or old age. If someone suddenly died, a person would say, "Gee, I just talked with her yesterday." Talking was synonymous with life. The person in question might have been ninety, and senile for twenty years, but she was alive to the neighborhood because she was seen and heard. If you could see her, you could ask her a serious question and get a serious answer.

The ladies were great at settling problems with their children and their grandchildren, but they were frightened of reading and books. Books were almost unavailable (except for "dirty" paperbacks). Only a handful of people had read a book within a five-block radius of my house. I would have thought that the Bible might have caught on. The only people who regularly read the Bible were the priests and nuns. So if the grandmothers decreed a pattern of behavior, they certainly didn't fear contradiction from a book or from any other form of the media for that matter. *Il Progresso*, the Italian-language newspaper, and the *Daily Mirror* (because of its racing coverage), and that was about it.

As a child, I was regularly warned about reading too much; if I did, I was told, I would go blind. Today, books have come into my home and friends' homes because the younger generation brings them into the house. The parents — my friends — allow books around. But when I was growing up books were treated gingerly. I can recall my grandmother going around our house picking up an occasional book that I had left lying around. She'd grab it by the end as if it were going to explode in her hand. That was a reflex that went back centuries, and her response was simply a reflection of the ingrained move. There was figuratively a ticking within that book. There was something about that book that she didn't like or understand. It could destroy, that much she was able to perceive.

The old ladies didn't rally around a substantive issue. They didn't clamor for an end to the Mafia; what the hell, their offspring were trying to get into the Mafiia. They weren't trying to get better schools. Most of the time they were talking about food. They did not talk about sex because, as I said, the subject was not mentionable. The only time in my memory when the subject was discussed by all of the old ladies throughout the neighborhood occurred just after the start of World War II. Tales of plunder and rape by the Japanese troops in the Philippines began filtering back. "They say they rape white women," said a woman named Rosa. I was too young to know what the word rape meant, but I did realize that all of the women were talking about it in both English and Italian. My mother was trying to feed my younger brother, who was sitting in a high chair, when still another of the ladies came around the screen door and yelled in, "They're a raping the white women. The white women." My mother got so upset that she smeared strained carrots all over my brother's face.

The subject that the old ladies completely took charge of was sex education. In fact, the first words out of Grandmother Roselli's mouth were *"Non toccare,"* which were pounded into every Italian boy's head from the age of six on. *Don't touch!* And that means you, grabbing yourself by the balls, which is what every generation of Italian boys has done since the founding of Rome. My friend Louis, one of Grandmother Roselli's grandsons, heard *non toccare* from the newly arrived grandmother and that was the extent of his sex education. "Don't touch" probably lasted right through the lifetime of these kids.

Since it was absolutely inconceivable that little girls would ever think of touching themselves, they were never yelled at. Only little boys got "no touch." In every Italian household, the grandmother laid down the basis of all the neuroses that were to follow. I have friends today who have eyes that can't stop twitching because their grandmothers kept saying, day after day, "Don't touch." There was no second step to the sex education. "Don't touch" came first and that was it. I would say that the old ladies set back Italian masturbation about five years.

Non Toccare as an inhibiting force kept the kids in check from the ages of six (if the kid was precocious) until eight or nine. And then, no matter what the grandmother said or did, the streets took over the education. I was a little slower than most about my sex education: my first hint of how babies were conceived came one day when a friend and I were traveling on the Sea Beach subway. Bobby drew on the side of the car a picture of a pregnant woman, complete with detailed baby in her stomach. I almost threw up, but then I felt: if this is what it takes to learn about sex, better grit my teeth and get on with it.

When I got home and tried to confirm what the Sea Beach train had told me, I got panicked looks from my parents. My grandparents absolutely washed their hands of the entire business. My parents were threatened by the questions: they would have to talk about something that was strictly forbidden in the home. The look and the phrase you got from any adult about sex was, "Don't ask me about that." "Don't ask me about that" and "Don't touch" were the cornerstones of Italian sex education.

Although "Don't ask me about that" began in my child-hood, the phrase has lasted all through my life. For example, if a forty-year-old woman wanted to ask her sixty-year-old mother how early menopause ran in their family, the mother (in between hot flashes) would glare at the daughter and say, "Don't ask me about that."

When daughters started to menstruate, the technique for educating them was, if anything, simpler than for the boys. The grandmother, with averted eyes, gave the grand-daughter a box of Kotex and that was that. My own wife, who went through exactly that, was told by her grand-mother, "You're lucky. When we were younger, we had to use rags."

The response to questions about sex and the Mafia was just about the same. If I asked my parents or my grand-parents why four bodies suddenly turned up three blocks away — "Was that the doing of the Mafia?" — the answer was, "We don't talk about that." I grant you the line is slightly different from "Don't ask me about that," but not by much. The Mafia was strictly fear. Knowledge about sex was way beyond fear — after all, there never was a question about bodily functions with the Mafia. My parents might whisper a story or two about the Mafia in the quiet confines of their bedroom late at night. But I seriously doubt they talked about s-x. I may be forty-one years old, but today in my parents' home the word, subject, and implications of sex are never discussed.

Since the neighborhood was very much isolated from information from the outside world, we picked up our knowledge as best we could. There was always a nineteen-year-old who had a vast amount of sexual experience. He would talk to a couple of kids who were sixteen or so.

The sixteen-year-olds would talk to a fourteen-year-old, but that's where the buck stopped. Kids of fourteen weren't about to share their knowledge with a measly twelve-year-old. Thus, good solid knowledge about sex remained pretty much a secret.

The movies were not much help either. They simply corroborated the "don't touch" instinct. Melvyn Douglas would kiss Rosalind Russell and everybody in the movie house would say, "Oh shit!" They certainly didn't do much touching in the cowboy movies. Abbott and Costello didn't touch.

And then breasts arrived in the neighborhood. The girls developed early in our tempestuous climate and our first impression was to stare and say, "My God, look at the nannas." "Nanna" was the neighborhood word for breasts, and we all used it. Masturbation followed breasts. Boys accidentally learned about rubbing themselves against coarse sheets at night. Nocturnal emissions were the first experience that most of us had. But there was no discussion with your family. Absolutely not even considered. The experience went to the street corner for discussion.

As to positions, and exactly how penises were inserted into vaginas, we turned to dirty comics — crude porn versions of Dagwood and Blondie, Popeye — and moved on to dog-eared dirty postcards and photographs, smudged and almost thumbed to death.

And then came the one book that managed to get into the neighborhood and cause a revolution: Irving Shulman's *Amboy Dukes*. It was published in 1947 and when it went into paperback even the nonreaders made a try at reading it. *The Amboy Dukes* was our generation's *God's Little Acre*. *The Amboy Dukes* was set in Brooklyn. It was tough for us to relate to a bunch of Georgia rednecks hanging around the farm, but we sure knew about street gangs in Brownsville — that was no more than twenty minutes away from us. Although Brownsville was Jewish, it was *us*. We had gangs, we had heard of the Brownsville gangs — what the hell, we knew guys like Mitch who were desperately trying to do whatever Mitch was doing to Betty in the book.

To this day, I can remember the sexy girl on the jacket, with her tremendous bosom. Approaching her from the shadows is a tough-looking guy. Her mouth is open either in anguish or ecstasy, take your pick. The book got passed around from guy to guy in school, and during lunch hour we sat around the schoolyard discussing it.

When we reached fourteen, the Church, in its infinite wisdom and its splendid greed, decided that we now were old enough to attend their youth "dances." The local churches would charge admission of a dime or fifteen cents and then sell soft drinks. The dances were for fourteen-year-olds on up, and usually were held on Friday night. The dances went from six to eight o'clock.

We all ran around in gangs when we were fourteen, and that included the girls. They weren't really gang gangs, but eighteen or twenty guys whose sense of organization consisted of buying the same kind of leather jackets. The girls' gang would consist of fifteen to sixteen girls and their jackets usually were of a cheap sateen material, with their names on the backs — like the Bopperettes.

There was always one gang member who, when hearing about a dance coming up, would say, very, very casually, "I think I'm going to go to the dance." He might have been fourteen *and a half*, which was indisputably older.

And so the whole gang went. That night, at dinner tables in the neighborhood, all of the gang members would inform their parents that they were going to a church dance. It wasn't as if we had to get permission; but we had to let people know where we would be. The guy who was bringing the entire gang with him usually said, "I'm going to the dance because I want to see Joan Pagino." And we all took our cue from that. We all told each other that the reason we were going to the dance was that we were going to see somebody we had been keeping our eye on.

I usually would wear my pegged powder-blue pants and my dark blue shirt and I'd spend a full hour on my hair, because in those days I had hair. At the church, there was one wary priest, one record player, and a record collection strictly from the 1940s. The dance was not unlike one of those prison movies with the guard (read priest) watching the exercise yard (read dance floor) very closely so that no fight broke out. At the age of fourteen, there were few fights over girls. But there might well be a fight over who bumped whom on the way to the Coke machine. Girls on one side, boys on the other, the area in between neutral territory. The music was playing, but no one was dancing. The boys would be digging elbows into each other; the girls would be giggling. And yet, the behavior wasn't so unusual: it mirrored the neighborhood.

Avenue U wasn't a neighborhood for social activity between adults. Two couples never went out on a weekend to a restaurant. Three or four young men never went out for a *sit-down* meal. Two young women, unmarried but in their twenties, would never have the nerve to go out by themselves in the neighborhood. People did not talk to one another.

After the dance, the girls walked out first, followed by the boys. They were showing off, but no suggestive or off-color remarks. Usually, we all went to a candy store after the dance. Although the boys and the girls really didn't confront one another at the candy store, the communication was slightly more advanced than the church dance. There may be one girl whom a guy is desperately trying to connect with, but he can't do it personally because that would be "going out" with her. So what he has to do is deal with the entire group but, in reality, talk to her.

We had to wing courtship; consequently there was a tremendous amount of mystery as well as fear about what we were supposed to do. If one of us didn't make some sort of move toward the girls — like showing off in front of them, or sort of talking to them — he was immediately called queer. We didn't know what a homosexual was either, until the entire neighborhood met its first homosexual in the first year at high school when we were introduced to a teacher named Bruce. There was no mistaking him, and we suddenly got the idea of what the real McCoy was.

There were one or two girls who would submit to group intercourse. It wasn't mass rape, because they went along with it willingly. I have often wondered about the girls because they always knew what was going on and what was in store for them.

There rarely was a problem of venereal disease or pregnancy because it was the era of the Trojan or the Ramses. I've always felt that the sale of Lifesavers was directly linked to the sale of Trojans. Here's a fifteen-year-old, about to have sex for the first time and shaking with fright, walking into a neighborhood drugstore trying to buy a pack of condoms. As he is about to open his mouth, in comes another customer and the kid immediately switches from the Trojan to a pack of Lifesavers. The other customer leaves, and the entire process begins again.

Today, in a drugstore, contraceptives are sold out in the open in wonderfully designed, hard-sell point-of-purchase displays. In those days, contraceptives were *always* in a mysterious drawer, which was always hidden way the hell away from the cash register.

I would walk into the drugstore, my eyes looking at my shoelaces, and mumble, "Pack of Trojans." At this point the clerk always lost part of his hearing. "What did you say? Trojans?" He usually said this in a voice that would reach out of the door and down to the corner. I'd usually look up at this point and see a woman who was a third cousin of my mother's approaching; my answer was a pack of Lifesavers. I never left the drugstore without three or four packs of the candy. They weren't such a hot product, but they had a wonderful thing going for them. The pharmacists weren't about to make it easy, either. I can remember, clear as a bell, their litany. "Yeah. We got Trojans. You want a dozen?" Said very loudly, again, with a big smirk. By this time I was usually through the floor and since everyone (including any customers who were in the store at the time) just knew you didn't need anywhere near a dozen, I'd take my pack of three Trojans and get out of the store.

We finally got a connection. A guy named Patsy, who grew up with us, got a job in Richie's Drugstore, and from then on we were able to walk in and buy contraceptives without too much trouble.

Girls who submitted to mass intercourse seemed to come

from families without brothers. They always had a sister or two and, in fact, one of the celebrated young women of the neighborhood had a twin who also liked to take on men by the gross.

The sexual act in these cases was always antisexual, obviously dehumanized, just as obviously male chauvinistic, and no fun for anyone. The girls always came from the lowest-level intelligence grading in the schools. (The high schools were broken down into classes from 9–1, the brightest, to 9–16, which meant the students could barely get their shoes tied. Most of the girls came from the 9–14 classes. They all had some psychological disturbance, and I am sure that what we indulged in did nothing to help their condition.)

These girls stuck together, because the youth community knew who they were even if the parents never did.

None of this took place in a convenient Holiday Inn. All of it, in good weather or bad, occurred in the schoolyard. In the winter, the girl and the guy were both wearing two or three coats. I've often thought how degrading it was for girl and boy. None of us knew any better. It was a degrading experience, that's for sure, and I am convinced that it psychologically crippled thousands of us in the years to come. But it was the way we lived and we had no one to tell us the damage caused by sex on the run and sex backed up against a cold concrete wall in a schoolyard.

There was *one* good experience out of all this. One day in public school — we were all in the ninth grade — a teacher named Tripani tried to educate us and made a bit of progress. The class was called hygiene, which was dumb because the one subject not covered by hygiene was the obvious one. We talked a lot about cleanliness of the feet and drying between the toes and things like that, but the taboo area between the knees and the chest wasn't discussed. One day a kid named John blurted out a question about venereal disease and Tripani looked staggered, and then walked to the door and shut it. He said, "I'm now going to talk to you about a lot of things, but if this talk gets out I could be thrown out of school and never teach again. But I'll answer any questions you guys have."

And the floodgates opened. The questions were as naive as "If you kiss a girl can she get pregnant?" This question from fifteen-year-olds in the ninth grade. We bombarded Tripani with everything we had wondered about for years. There were four or five in the class who led the way in asking the questions. The rest of us just sat there and soaked it up. It was the first — and, as it turned out, the last — bit of sex education any of us ever had before becoming completely taken over by the streets, and I'm glad we got it. It's amazing that if the weather had been better that day we wouldn't have had the lecture because most of the time the hygiene class went outside for calisthenics. As for Tripani, I don't know where he is today, or even if he is still alive. But he certainly struck a blow for education that one day in ninth-grade hygiene.

After the church dances we continued our relationships with girls in our candy stores. We had plenty of candy stores. There had to be enough of them to take care of the betting population, the cardplayers, and the kids on the make. In each candy store group there would be about fifteen guys and maybe five or six girls.

There still was unbelievably strict supervision of daughters by their fathers. "My daughter is a virgin, she's not going to risk it in a candy store," one father who was an uncle of mine said. When that father walked down the aisle, his daughter wore legitimate white, no crossed fingers behind the back. Many fathers would not let their daughters hang around the candy store. Only the most "liberal" of parents would allow their daughters out, and both the girls and the fathers were looked upon with disfavor.

The moment all of us started our candy store phase, the neighborhood grandmothers washed their hands of us. "How dare they leave the home" was the comment. The grandmothers always predicted doom and destruction without one word about sex.

There was no such formalized structure as a "date," but girls began to dress with care and awareness of the boys. The boys were beginning to understand that there were some girls they wanted to be with. The curious thing about the candy store gang was that not much really went on. Our crew consisted of fifteen guys and Judy, Maria, Laura, and a couple of other girls. We all hung around Louie's, sitting in the five booths along the side of the store or congregated outside the booths. And we were in there from three-thirty (school was out at three o'clock) until five or five-thirty. Home for dinner and then back to the candy store from seven o'clock until nine or ten. The store usually stayed open until eleven o'clock or so.

As we sat next to each other, there was no physical contact between boy and girl. The girls almost became "one of the guys" in that kind of atmosphere, and I can't recall any one of the girls ever marrying a guy from her candy store group. As the group started to outgrow the candy store and disintegrate at the age of eighteen or so, the girls went through a very bad period of loneliness. Then they'd get a job at the local savings bank or insurance company, meet a guy, and get married.

When it came to sexual preferences and styles, you must remember this was a Victorian age. We were our father's children, and when the boys sat and talked about sex there were staggering gaps in their knowledge. The missionary position was the only position they ever had heard of, except for a few perverse French postcards, and we certainly didn't trust the French when it came to sex. And any other arcane pleasures beyond the pornographic comic books and the postcards were simply beyond our range of thinking. We just couldn't handle anything else.

The movies were a vehicle for meeting and coming in contact with the opposite sex, after the candy store. And then we got wheels. We were sixteen and seventeen and the movies were the best place to pick up girls. In those days we had the Kingsway, the Avalon, the Mayfair, the Stillwell, the Dewey. The Dewey was tiny: today it's a small appliance store. We never saw the movies themselves. We were constantly shifting, from aisle to aisle, in search of the perfect girl. There were different grades of movie houses and, obviously, different grades of girls in those movie houses. I found a much better class of girl at the Kingsway instead of the Dewey, which was content with gangster movies and cowboy features that had to be at least third run.

In all of the movie houses, the pickups were upstairs and the married folks were downstairs. Essentially, the movies were our Maxwell's Plum, except that some idiot was trying to show a movie during the mating game. Today I'm seeing movies all the way through for the first time on late-night television, the same movies that were shown at the Kingsway. The other night I watched something called *The Tender Trap* with Debbie Reynolds and Frank Sinatra. I vaguely remembered the opening credits of the movie. And I can recall the ending, which had Reynolds and Sinatra walking off together in the sunset, but I sure as hell don't remember a thing in between. What was I doing? Obviously, on a search throughout the movie house trying to find a girl.

We would change our seats twenty or thirty times during a double feature, and if we were lucky enough to find somebody, up we went to the top of the balcony. You didn't talk or laugh it up in the balcony, because some pretty heavy petting was taking place. One day when I was up there a guy I knew named Lefty was literally screwing a girl and an usher told the guy to stop. Lefty didn't stop, not believing in *coitus interruptus cinemata*. The usher persisted, and finally Lefty got up, pulled on his pants, and then threw the usher down the stairs, injuring him severely. The cops took Lefty away and booked him on felonious assault charges; the hospital took the usher away with a wrenched back and contusions; and the girl was sent home, presumably frustrated.

Although the movies were fertile fields, the street corners along Ocean Parkway were the best places for boy to meet girl. As we reached our eighteenth birthdays we reached automobiles, no matter how rickety. In the spring, summer, and fall, girls would congregate on corners of Ocean Parkway, which, if you go out to Brooklyn today, is still being used as a giant mixer. Five girls would be sitting on a bench (Ocean Parkway was conveniently built with islands on either side of the main roadway, giving people a chance to sit down on benches). A car with three or four guys would drift by, and a guy would stick his head out the window and say, "Hey." That was the standard, if crude, greeting used, and it had a strong guttural tone to it.

Occasionally, traffic problems took the enjoyment out of the mating game. Dozens of cars were cruising around, filled with young guys who one day were dreaming of playing shortstop for the Dodgers and the next day wanted only to get their hands on a woman. Certain streets in Gravesend had rights to certain corners on Ocean Parkway. Once in a while a carload from West Eleventh Street would feel that their particular corner had been encroached on by a carload from West Ninth Street. Then there would be a hell of a fight.

During the summer we also had the beaches to roam, from Coney Island to Far Rockaway. I met my wife, Barbara, at the beach. She was fifteen and lived about ten minutes away from me. After I had gone out with her for a year I realized that I had to come to terms with the problem of telling my parents what was going on. I just couldn't come right out and say, "Hey, Mom, I got this terrific new girl I've been seeing some time." The neighborhood could not stand being direct. Usually, when a guy went with a girl for a year or so, he would then begin to set his family up.

I did the same thing. One night I said, "Gee, it's great at Coney Island, we really had a great time." A week passed by and the next Sunday I went to the beach again.

My mother said, "You'll need some sandwiches, won't you?"

"No, I don't think I'll need any sandwiches, there're

plenty of sandwiches at the beach," I said. I got a strange look but no hard questions.

A week after that I came back from the beach and said, "Wow, I had a terrific pastrami sandwich at the beach today." My parents' antennae went up.

"Pastrami? Pastrami? Who brings pastrami to the beach? What's her name?"

"Ah, Linda," I said. "Linda brought pastrami sandwiches to the beach."

Suddenly, that great cloud of fear rose in the house. "My God, my son is with a girl who is Jewish." Pastrami equals Jewish and if he's with such a girl, there's the family, the house, the whole thing; "We'll have to move back to Italy."

I explained that Linda was my friend Ronnie's girl, who wasn't Jewish but Irish, she lived on Kings Highway and Flatbush Avenue, and she just happened to like pastrami. "Anyhow," I said, "I don't eat the pastrami sandwiches. I eat eggplant parmigiana sandwiches." Another country heard from.

My mother grilled me some more. "Who goes to the trouble of making you eggplant parmigiana just for the beach?" My mother knew the eggplant parmigiana was a production, first cooking the eggplant in breadcrumbs, then putting the whole thing together and baking it in the oven for about an hour. Her interest was piqued. "Linda, the pastrami girl, also makes the eggplant?" Homing in.

"No," I told her. "There's this other girl at the beach who brings the eggplant. Her name is Barbara, and she's very nice."

I played it cool for a few months until we were in the

dead of winter. I couldn't casually talk about sandwiches I was going to take to the beach. "I'm going out, Ma." "Where?" "Oh, I thought I'd go to the movies." I then told my mother that I was going to the movies with a girl named Barbara, the same Barbara whom I had mentioned about five months before — the eggplant parmigiana girl. By this time, I'd been dating Barbara for about two years.

After my disclosure to my mother, she never said anything to my father. Nor did she ask any tough questions to my face either. And then one day I really got my courage up and asked her if she'd like to meet Barbara. She shrugged and nodded. The next move was up to me, but I had to pick the appropriate time.

All over the neighborhood friends of mine were coping with the same problem: talking like mature adults to their parents for the first time in their lives. When you break the steel umbilical cord in an Italian household you don't just get scissors — you've got to use a torch.

And then one day there was a death in the family. My father's mother died, which meant a funeral, and funerals were ideal occasions to quietly introduce someone to the family.

I was using the funeral almost as a football player uses a blocking back. The funeral took some of the pressure off the meeting between Barbara and my parents. Funerals are times for a gathering of people; they are extremely helpful when you're trying to introduce a girl to your parents.

The meeting went off very well, because Italians are very impressed with people who come to funerals. "They show respect," my mother used to say, and since the Italian's world is circumscribed by respect (family, mother, Church,

Mafia), anyone who showed up at a stranger's funeral was safely within the boundaries. Admittedly, I could have brought a deviate to a funeral and to most of the people at the funeral the deviate would be showing a "lot of respect." My mother was very pleased with the turn of events. It took her mind off the funeral. She and Barbara sized each other up and my mother's comment later was, "She's very tall." Since my mother is about four foot eight, anything higher than a breadbox is very tall, but those were code words meaning "She's okay. If you want to go ahead and someday marry her, she will be accepted." Very important. So all things considered it was a very good funeral. The body got buried; but another life got started and who could ask for more?

There were very good vibes at the funeral and my mother was thinking, "Not only did I get a chance to meet Barbara, but the entire family got a look at her, too." Barbara was very nervous, and so was I.

Although Barbara was from a slightly different neighborhood, she was from Brooklyn, she was Italian, Catholic, and so on. All of us in Gravesend married within these boundaries except for a guy in the neighborhood named Gaetano. He met a girl at a dance and she was from somewhere called Yorkville, and he went and married her. Immediately, we began hearing tales from the bowels of Eighty-sixth Street in Manhattan about the strange tribal doings of the Germans. Gaetano came back to the neighborhood a couple of times, told us about knife-carrying citizens of that strange borough, and never returned to our shore.

But the guys in the neighborhood were conformists from the beginning. They never did anything that did not conform to the neighborhood's code. The code was rigid and we didn't break the code; the code broke us. I never could come waltzing in the screen door saying, "Hi Mom, I just met this terrific black girl and we're going to be married." Or Protestant girl. Or Irish girl. Or Jewish girl. Or anything ("Hi, Mom, I just met this terrific Italian guy named Freddie . . .").

My friends today have simply grown into carbon copies of their parents. Barbara and I had three children, never once mentioning to our parents that the children arrived via something other than the stork. My parents became grandparents, but not through sex.

When I was growing up my friends and I tried so hard to imitate our parents. We didn't want to disappoint them. I can still remember guys in their twenties talking about certain aspects of sex and saying, "Ugh. That's disgusting! Filthy." These are people who devoutly believed that black men were sexually superior, Jewish women were sexually superior, and the Irish only liked to drink. They never ranked the Italian male or female.

White Anglo-Saxon Protestants were unheard of. The neighborhood didn't even know there was such a thing as a WASP. (Many years later, when my partner and I hired our first non-Italian, my partner came to me and said, "We've got our first WASP." I said, "Terrific." Both of us were wrong. He happened to be Irish and we still didn't know the difference.)

There wasn't too much of a problem about bad media influence. The Legion of Decency made sure we didn't see any offensive movies, and in those days the Legion really counted for something when they issued their condemned list.

The people in the neighborhood didn't know what sex was. A friend of mine named Pete once admitted that he'd "slept" with three women in his entire life: he'd been number twenty in a schoolyard lineup; he'd made it with a girl in the back seat of a car; and then he got married at the age of eighteen. How could you have secret desires of sex if the entire neighborhood grew up with dirty versions of Dagwood Bumstead and Blondie? The women had an even more difficult time. They *never* had another man. They might have gone to bed with their husbands-to-be at an early age, but then they always married the same fellow. Always.

The confessional always got the emotional garbage from our lives. How in God's name the priests ever sorted it out I'll never know. Well, I do know: they didn't sort it out. All they did was nod and absolve.

In my neighborhood, the belief was that Italian women have but two purposes in life: to get married and to make a reasonable meat sauce. In Gravesend, the concept of holy matrimony was drilled into girls' heads from the age of four or five on. And it hasn't changed, in Brooklyn or Queens or Staten Island or pockets of the Bronx. It may never change.

There were two great and tenacious forces at work to preserve and protect the integrity and the virginity of the Italian maiden: the Church and the Italian father.

Just go over to my old neighborhood on a Wednesday, and hang around a public school and watch what happens at 3:00 P.M. Kids come out of the public school and head for the local church for "religious instruction." Religious instruction is not what it seems to be. Little boys and girls are told they have been put on this earth to get married and to propagate. And thus will the church grow. Forget all those reports that say the Church is losing members and money because of its backward stand on birth control. Concentrate on what they're impressing on those pliable minds: get married.

The Church shouldn't take all the blame. The parents are in there, too, in spades, pushing the concept of marriage as if it were the sole alternative in life. The only kind of dolls given to little Italian girls are bride dolls. A cry of joy is heard in an Italian household when a little girl shows her parents she knows how to dress the little doll.

For those people who are wondering if this is the dark ages and where in heaven's name is women's liberation and haven't the people been brought into the twentieth century, the answers, in no particular order, are: "Yes, it is the dark ages; no, the people aren't aware of the twentieth century; and women's liberation evidently got held up at the Brooklyn-Battery tunnel."

The average "courtship" lasts anywhere from three to five years, starting at the age of fifteen or so and culminating in marriage at the age of twenty or twenty-one. Full planning of the wedding begins about a year and a half before the ceremony. In some large Italian families the negotiations over seating arrangements and invitation lists may take eight months. Next to funeral parlors and automobile junkyards, catering halls for weddings are our third-ranking industry.

After the age of twenty-one, things start going downhill for the women. My neighborhood tolerates a single girl until that age, but after that she is on her way to becoming an old maid. In this respect, the neighborhood is very much like Sicily.

That stage of development during which the women of the family leave the home, go off to college, move to the big city, have an affair or two, and perhaps get married at the age of twenty-six or twenty-seven is absolutely unknown to Italian women. They don't go to college, or if they do it certainly is within commuting distance from the home. Emblazoned on the brains of all Italian fathers is the churchly message: Thou shalt not let thy virgin daughters out of sight for more than twenty-four hours at a time — evil might transpire.

The community pressure also begins at twenty-one, consisting of unpleasant comments and digs at women who haven't married. "Why are you dating so much? Why aren't you married like everybody else? Look at Ella Turnesa down the block. She's married." On and on it goes, unrelenting and often vicious.

The age of twenty-seven is just about the cutoff point. If a woman hasn't married by then she's relegated to taking care of Mama in Mama's old age: the unmarried daughter, a classic in Italian households.

And it's not just the family that's putting in its two cents worth about the girl not getting married. Everyone — storekeepers, priests, and the entire social structure — is hammering away with the litany, "Get married, you've got to get married, you've got to get married."

The problem with the community — a problem that exists to this day — was that it was not structured for young people to meet each other. From the ages of thirteen through twenty, boys could meet girls in one of four places: the school, the church, the beach, and Ocean Parkway. A young woman could be picked up at one of these places without fear of censure. This carefully controlled courtship lasted only until the first couple in the group got married.

Then it seemed as if an avalanche struck; the entire group "grew up" and got married. "Hanging around" streets suddenly was beneath us. One couple got married; the rest of that particular group started marrying with a vengeance. The first marriage took place before the man reached twenty-one.

The familial pressures within the Italian structure are almost impossible for the outsider to comprehend. In our family there was a cousin, Susan, who was pressured and pressured until she reached the age of twenty-four or so. At twenty-four the family said the hell with it; she was doomed to live out her life as an old maid.

In fact, the word about Susan was, "All she wants is to have 'fun.'" In this case, "fun" meant having more than one man to date. "Fun" was laughing, enjoying herself, having a good time. "Look at her, all she wants to do is to have 'fun'; she'll never get married." (In this context, virginity was the constant; nobody ever questioned that.)

However, Susan fooled everyone in the family — she had her "fun" until the advanced age of twenty-six and then she got married. Susan married Orsini, also from Gravesend, but then they wisely moved to Houston and reportedly are very happy.

These same pressures are still operative in my neighborhood today; although they might not be exercised with such a vengeance, fathers don't change, haven't changed, and probably won't change in the future.

I am invited to weddings of young people who are eighteen, nineteen, in their early twenties. The family and society pressures are still the same: get married, have children, take root, die.

The only ways in which Italians are united or reunited are at funerals and at weddings. A good example of this is my friend Larry's sister, Emma, who tried to break with tradition. At the age of nineteen she decided to move out of her family's house into her own apartment. She worked in an office in downtown Brooklyn and her plan was to get an apartment in Brooklyn Heights, which would be much closer to her job.

Mistakenly, Emma thought her family had moved into the twentieth-century world. She was wrong. When she approached her family they were stunned. Not just her father, although he was particularly shocked, but the entire family. They all called her a whore (pronounced "hoor"); and that is the specific word they used.

Beyond calling his daughter a whore, her father disowned her. In the family, that girl had died, was forgotten, was punished. "No daughter of mine is going to leave this house unless she leaves it with a wedding gown on," was the way her father put it.

My feeling is that her family's reaction was no different from the response that would have been made forty-four years ago.

But, in being officially "dead," Emma still hadn't given up *her* interest and desire to be in the family structure. So she had to find herself a family connection — literally — a source who could fill her in on what the family was doing. Emma had done this, and then one day she heard, through her connection, that an uncle had died. She knew that she had to go to the funeral and she knew that when she got there her father would not look at her if he spotted her, but rather would turn his head.

She never made it to the funeral home. Emma got pneumonia and wound up in the hospital. She was in no danger of dying but was really sick. And now comes the part I referred to about Italians being reunited at funerals and weddings (and calamities).

Father was told about the pneumonia and he hurried to her side. I'd like to say they had a tear-filled reunion at the hospital, but they didn't. It was awkward, and consisted mainly of the father asking questions about her condition. Nobody made mention of the fact that Emma had been exiled from her family and had not spent a Thanksgiving or a Christmas Day with them in two years. At the end of her hospitalization, her father picked her up and took her *to her own apartment.*

Her father took her back into the family on a *conditional basis.* The conditions are that Emma can live in her apartment; the family will welcome her (distantly) to family meals and gatherings; but if she ever falls from grace again, for whatever reason, she is off the books for good. By the way, Emma was twenty-one when she got sick and she, too, was considered beyond marriage and doomed to be an old maid for life.

We have not regressed to the point where we hang out the bloody sheets the day following the wedding, but we still insist that the bride wear white when she walks down the aisle with her father. The younger generations make a big deal about moving away to the suburbs, learning the new way of doing things, but we still put on the weddings.

Follow me for a moment: if the daughter lives at home,

then the family is there to protect the prize. If the daughter willingly says she will stay at home until she is married, then she is consciously going along with the charade. The girl who lives at home knows that her father, her mother, or her weird uncle will always be in attendance when a young man comes to the door to pick her up for a date.

Culture shock is the look on the face of a twenty-seven- or twenty-eight-year-old guy from a different neighborhood as he brings home the vestal virgin from a night out and suddenly encounters the entire family waiting up. The father is sitting there in a faded seersucker robe. The look on his face says in no uncertain terms: God help you if you touched my daughter.

The Italians are unique in many respects and one of those is that they are the only group of immigrants who came to this country and never allowed *any* of the social customs or mores to rub off on them. The Irish, the Jews, the Germans, the Poles, all of them have learned the language and assimilated. The Italians have *pretended* that they've assimilated, but it just isn't true. Walk through Mulberry Street, go to Astoria in Queens, travel to Clove Lake in Staten Island, and the message is loud and clear and usually the same: do not change and adopt the heathen ways of the aliens.

I'm not kidding. Phil, one of the guys I grew up with, has a daughter of twenty. Phil left the neighborhood, ostensibly to raise his family in better surroundings. The daughter went to college because she thought her father wanted her to go to college. She studied merchandising because that sounded like a good way to meet a husband; in fact, she worked in a department store while she was going to school.

Well, she studied hard, did well, and her friends held a "shower" for her just the other day to celebrate her forthcoming marriage at the age of twenty. The pattern is very clear; she'll become pregnant within eleven months and the cycle will keep going on and on. And, by the way, she's very happy about it all; if anyone questions her about the inevitability of it all, she shrugs and says she's delirious with joy. And so is Phil. She is, when you talk to her for any length of time, very proud of what she's accomplished: getting through two years of college (without understanding a thing she learned), catching a husband, not being considered "loose" by anyone's standards, and about to become a mother. She sounded like a little old lady when I talked to her, and I realized that although she was physically out of my neighborhood, the neighborhood hadn't really left her at all.

To my way of thinking, there is something very strange about a group of people who never let a fresh idea in. I can imagine a Jewish father being upset at his daughter's leaving home and moving into an apartment, but drumming her out of the family? Never. That man who wrote Emma off is, to all intent and purpose, a very nice guy, but who knows what kind of corroded things are in his head?

About Phil's daughter just out of college and about to be married. I ought to mention along the way that when I say it will be eleven months until she's pregnant I'm no more than three weeks off on the timing. But no way is she pregnant now and being forced into a marriage. There were no such things as shotgun weddings in my neighborhood, and there are no such things now. Maybe in funny Italian movies set near Naples the bride shows up at the church as big as a house. But not on Avenue U. The reason is simple — all the people at the party after the baby has been born have their hands underneath the tables. And what they're doing with their hands is pretty simple. They're using their fingers to count the months. There is a lot of finger-counting at Italian parties. A lot of innocent smiles and questions like: "When were you married?"

Of course there are premature births. But what the hell, this goes on even in normal societies. The point about the Italians is that the planning starts a good year and a half before the event. And conception being what it is, there have been occasions when the entire engagement/wedding has been speeded up. But no one is forced to get married; there are no Marcello Mastroiannis with twitches being dragged to the altar. Boy and girl (I hesitate to say man and woman) are willingly dashing up to the altar. The moment the engagement is announced, that's it: the commitment has been made, virtue has been rewarded.

When my group was getting married and making plans, the first thing a couple had to do was hire the band. Meyer Davis may have been big in debutante circles in New York and Palm Beach. Eddie Caso was very big with Italians in Brooklyn, Eddie was the first successful franchise operation to hit Brooklyn, even before McDonald's and Colonel Sanders. Because Caso was a nice Italian name.

I must have attended at least one hundred Eddie Caso weddings in my youth. Nobody ever laid eyes on Eddie Caso. For all I know he was a wise-guy booking agency in the Brill Building, sending out hundreds of five-man bands consisting of saxophone, drums, a guy with a cornet who doubled on strange instruments like triangles, an accordion, and maybe, if the wedding was a little home-style, a piano.

Even a year before the wedding, after you locked Eddie

Caso into place, you had to sign up for Robert Grasso. He was the Court Photographer of Brooklyn. He also had dozens, maybe hundreds, of photographers working for him taking pictures of *the day*. The bride getting dressed, the bridegroom's mother crying, the bride's mother sobbing, the whole show. The photographs would carry you right through the day, including the departure for the honeymoon in Miami. The sad thing about Robert Grasso was he was found one day with enough bullet holes in him to kill him at least three times. I always felt he got caught taking pictures of the honeymoon instead of the wedding.

In Gravesend, money often was a very real consideration, so there was a very elaborate scale of weddings worked out. At the bottom of the scale was the "at home football." Football weddings got their name from the fact that the main source of nourishment was sandwiches, made ahead of time, consisting usually of cheese, prosciutto or provolone, and wrapped in waxed paper. The living room was cleared and two tables were set up at either end of the room. And then thousands of sandwiches would be heaped on the two tables. Each table was manned by a guy who had the skills of Johnny Lujak of Notre Dame.

As the guests started to jam the room, the sandwiches would get grabbed up with a vengeance. If the guy watching table number one suddenly was hit for a flock of ham sandwiches and he ran short and didn't have the time to open up another carton, he simply yelled across the room to guy number two: "Hey, gimme half a dozen prosciutto" (in their haste vowels also got dropped on the floor, thus prosciutto became "proshoot"). Guy number two would grab six prosciutto and literally hurl them across the room, over the heads of the guests, right into the arms of guy number one. The sandwiches were thrown not unlike a forward pass; and they were caught not unlike a spiraling football. (Of course you had problems like interception, just as in real football games. People not satisfied with the thickness of one sandwich would take to intercepting a sandwich or two as it arched across the room.)

One step up from the "at home football" wedding was the "away football" wedding, which simply meant that the wedding reception was held in a rented hall rather than in the family's home. Rented hall really doesn't get across the idea of the simplicity of these affairs. The big hall in terms of desirability in our neighborhood was the empty floor above the post office.

Wedding receptions held in halls were characterized by sandwiches and hundreds of little kids sliding all over the waxed floors and knocking over elderly relatives. Italians would consider it an insult if the host had said, "Please leave the kids at home." First of all, there wasn't anybody at home to leave the kids with; the whole family was diving for provolone sandwiches. Second, an Italian figures the bride and groom have some nerve telling him to keep his kids home. So it's chaos. Some families with seventeen children (and I'm not exaggerating) would take up entire tables, people would be slipping on loose salami on the floor, and most of the kids older than eight would drink behind their parents' backs and then throw up.

One step up from the football wedding came the catered weddings–main dish chicken — which were held at a succession of Brooklyn catering halls designed to accommodate a maximum number of people in as uncomfortable a manner as possible. One of the most prominent catering halls in our neighborhood was called Ralph's, and during that short period of time when I was aware of such things and still living in Brooklyn, Ralph's burned to the ground at least twenty-three times. It led the league in Brooklyn for number of suspicious fires. It would burn down at the end of one June wedding season and stay burned down until the start of the next year's June wedding season. On July 1, if it hadn't burned by that date, the fire trucks in the neighborhood would make a run by the place and practically wait for the spontaneous combustion to begin.

Anyhow, Ralph's specialized in catered weddings and they made only one error in all of the years they served the community. At one wedding — it happened to have been one of my cousins — the management tried to institute something new to my neighborhood: a buffet wedding. Ralph's figured that they'd save on hiring waiters and other help, and simply put all of the food out in an attractive display and let people take what they wanted.

It went down in the books as the biggest disaster ever to hit Ralph's. Gravesend simply wasn't ready for the *concept* of a buffet; well, ready isn't quite the word — they really didn't know what to do with it. There were dozens of little old Italian men running from one end of the buffet table to the other muttering curses in Italian and saying in English, "What kind of a place is this, with the food all piled up and the bread all piled up and nobody has taken the trouble to put it into sandwiches?" If an old uncle is raised to expect sandwiches in waxed paper at a wedding, he's going to be thrown by the sight of plain meat and cheese without bread.

Forgetting buffets, the step beyond catered wedding– main dish chicken was catered wedding–main dish roast beef with imitation Italian food thrown in as an afterthought. Squishy ravioli and so forth. As the years have gone by our neighborhood has moved from strictly beer (mostly with the football wedding, home), to Seagrams 7, Four Roses, Three Feathers, and booze of that ilk, to today where a lot of really terrible New York State nonvintage champagne is poured.

Real class is a cocktail hour before the catered roast beef. The timetable, therefore, runs something like this: the wedding ceremony itself is at three o'clock at the church. Three always has been the hot hour and couples book the church at least a year in advance to make sure of their time slot. Since the bridesmaids are selected at just about the same time the engagement is announced, the color of the gowns the bridesmaids are wearing is also known in advance. When I would arrive at the church and was suddenly hit by four weddings going on at the same time and I couldn't for the life of me remember the name of the bride, I usually could remember the color of the bridesmaids' gowns. "Green bridesmaids, that's us."

The ceremony is no more than fifteen minutes and out unless the daughter happens to be related to a big contributor to the church.

After the ceremony, over to Robert Grasso for the wedding-party photographs, which take some time. Finally, to Ralph's Catering for the big dinner. It's now about five o'clock and everybody is herded into a small room off the main banquet room for cocktails and hors d'oeuvres.

Finally, everyone is there, and the crowd moves into the main hall, where the dramatics begin. Eddie Caso's group is ready and suddenly the lights dim, there is a loud drum roll and crash of cymbals, and the master of ceremonies (who doubles on sax) starts to introduce the bridesmaids and the ushers. "And now let's hear it for Angela and Gino," cries the saxophonist. (Gino is also the betrothed of Angela.) Then we have Vincent and Maryann, and on it goes until, "And now, ladies and gentlemen, for the first time as man and wife, Rocco and Catherine . . ." Big cheer, tears, the band is coping with "Here Comes the Bride," and everyone finds his or her place on the dais so the toasts can begin.

It is axiomatic at an Italian wedding that the main toast is usually given by the bridegroom's brother, and he is often drunk and incoherent. Up until now he has never made a public appearance, much less a public speech. He never again will be asked to make a speech before more than two people. This is it, for him, and in typical fashion he manages to fuck it up. One public speech in a lifetime, and the speech is no more than fifteen words long. The family has written all fifteen words out for him and he manages to forget seven of the fifteen.

It is a total disaster. "To my brother, uh, and his, uh, wife, uh, I just want to say you both are, uh, good kids." This coming from a guy who is maybe two years younger than the bride and groom. "Uh, you're both good kids and you deserve a lot of, uh, little ones, and I want to thank my brother and his girl, uh, I mean his wife, uh . . ." On it goes and the strange thing is nobody is yelling at him to sit down. On the contrary, everyone is very respectful watching this guy die like a salami on the dais.

After about five minutes the brother sits down to uproarious applause, and everyone on the dais reaches over to touch him and say, "Hey, very nice, Tony, very nice." Tony modestly accepts congratulations and grasps at his collar like an asphyxiated pike. The band stirs restlessly.

A couple of other toasts are made, also incoherent, incomprehensible, and weird. At this point, the bride requests *her song* to be played by Eddie Caso and the boys.

The band then segues into "Mr. Wonderful," which was the title song of a dreadful Broadway show of the 1950s starring Sammy Davis, Jr. It is burned into the memories of millions of people who have attended Italian weddings that when "Mr. Wonderful" is played, the bridegroom staggers from the dais with a sleazy grin on his face and starts dancing with his mother. Then the bride's father dances with the bride to the tune of "Daddy's Little Girl." Depending on the size of the band and its musicians' ambition, they might attempt to do "Mr. Wonderful" *and* "Daddy's Little Girl" simultaneously. I've personally seen this attempted several times and it has never failed to move me. Obviously, one of the songs is going to be a little heavy on the rhythm and blues side of the band, but certainly no one at the reception will notice anything like that. Only at Italian weddings are two songs played at once. Meyer Davis wouldn't have the nerve. The concept of the bride dancing with her father and the bridegroom with his mother is an image that touches all Italian bases. To make the picture complete, I can safely say that during the dancing of "Daddy's Little Girl" it never fails that Daddy weeps copiously, tears streaming down his joyful cheeks, and when the band sees that the ducts are working they really throw themselves into their work.

One last musical note. There is always plenty of amateur talent at Italian weddings, people who knew they should have tried out at the Metropolitan Opera auditions but never got around to it. This vast untapped pool of talent comes to the surface during weddings. About three-quarters of the way through the wedding reception they'll stagger up to the podium and inform the band leader that they're going to sing either "Come Back to Sorrento" or "Mama."

Since the band has a long history of dealing with drunks, they know they have to let the guy sing at least one song. Anything less is a riot; anything more is a disaster. And sing he does, hitting about two out of five notes, but with a hell of a lot of *brio*. Don't think that the people at the reception are in favor of amateur night — not at all. They're generally mortified that Cousin Willie is making such an ass of himself and everyone present looks down at either his plate or his shoes.

After "Come Back to Sorrento," a stunned silence fills the catering hall, and the emcee, desperate to lift the level of depression, has the band break into "Hatikva." Now, the Italians don't know that this is a Jewish song; in fact, not one Jew is on the premises. But the Italians do know that you dance to the tune and they all are acquainted with the melody. And so, with the emcee prodding them, the entire room breaks into a hora, which is a pretty funny notion. From the hora they progress to the tarantella, which is at least in the right ethnic pew.

Although the older ladies, the aunts and elderly non-married cousins, love the dances, the older men despise them. Any man over the age of thirty-five is by now either standing outside the hall or he's down in the bathroom. I have attended weddings and walked into the bathroom to find ten relatives of mine (including six uncles) standing around the bathroom listening as the emcee has all the old ladies going "You put your left foot out." The men all are wearing their one suit, basic blue, with their new (for the occasion) white-on-white shirt whose collar is so heavily starched that it is cutting right through the back of their necks. They're not used to crowds and/or social situations, and they're especially not used to ties. In fact, they don't wear ties. For the most part, their ties are pulled way off the side of their shirt collars and usually the shirts are unbuttoned halfway down their chests. These are the bride's uncles, the groom's uncles, and the older cousins who don't amount to much. Contrary to popular belief, Italians really aren't that crazy about music, and when Eddie Caso is amplified to such a degree that the uncles' teeth rattle, they all seek refuge in the bathroom.* Eddie will turn the amplifiers down as soon as the first aunt faints from the sound.

Basically, Italian men don't like weddings that much. They don't go out at all, and if they have to go out, they'd prefer attending a funeral, where everything is low-keyed and a lot better suited to their taste. At the wedding, there are embarrassing confrontations, relatives whom they'd rather not run into, people they just don't want to see. After killing as much time as possible in the bathroom, they congregate outside the catering hall, walking around and talking baseball among themselves.

This kind of behavior — this edgy, barely-making-it kind of attitude — is prevalent at a neighborhood wedding. God forbid that the wedding be held outside the neighborhood. I once had to attend a wedding held at the old St. George Hotel in downtown Brooklyn. It had to be about a half hour from my neighborhood; it could have just as easily been ten light-years away.

The mother of a friend of mine who attended that wedding

---

* The average uncle at a wedding spends more time with his penis hanging out than the groom does during his entire first year of marriage.

was so nervous about the whole thing that she stole a gigantic silver (well, silver-plated at least) coffeepot from the banquet and sneaked it out in a shopping bag at the end of the evening. I don't think she's a klepto or anything like that; she simply was nervous about the wedding, and one of the ways she reacted was to swipe the coffeepot.

That wedding at the St. George caused a lot of negative comment in the neighborhood. The bride came from a neighborhood family, and they were fairly simple people, in modest circumstances. The guy's family also came from the neighborhood, but his father had made a lot of money, the source of which nobody could pinpoint. We never talked about the rackets or anything, but his money had a peculiar tinge to it. And it was the bridegroom's father, with his money, who pushed for the St. George Hotel and offered to pay the tab. As far as the people in the neighborhood were concerned, the family of the bridegroom was "putting on airs" and of course "the bride and groom are never going to be happy." The people in the neighborhood were not attending a wedding at a hall called Château de something-or-other; the St. George was a totally different world.

In a way, the neighborhood gossips were quite prophetic about that couple. The guy turned out to be something of a wasted character, as did his wife. And, like practically all young Italian couples, they immediately started to eat like crazy the minute the ceremony was over and gained about eighty pounds each.

There seems to be a syndrome — for both man and woman — that the moment they get back from the honeymoon they start to devour food. They take care of their bodies fairly well until the wedding; the next day, though, stuff those mouths. As far as the woman is concerned, the day that license is signed, sealed, and delivered, the sky's the limit. Life is absolutely over for her. All she has left to do is eat, sleep, and bear children. She's been told to get married and she got married. And that's it. It's the couple's mission in life and they've done what their parents, the neighborhood, and the Church have been telling them all this time: they got married. So all they do now is eat. They eat cakes as if they were communion wafers: on the tongue and a moment later an entire cake is gone.

The nice thing about the wedding scene is that there rarely is any trouble about whether the bride married someone "inferior" to her. There never were any so-called caste problems. No one in Gravesend ever really married beneath his or her station. Actually, everyone was inferior and, correspondingly, everyone had an inferiority complex.

Also, we never had any problem about anyone marrying outside of the Church. You might marry someone who didn't give a damn about the Church but all of us began in the Church. To my knowledge, no one in the neighborhood ever married a Protestant. And if someone was Jewish, forget it. A distant cousin of mine married a Jewish woman. She converted to Catholicism to get married, so, in the eyes of the Church, the Jewish bit was long gone. And of course my family completely blocked the fact that she was Jewish. It's one of the first collective blocks in the history of the neighborhood. Today, if I were to innocently ask my mother if my family had any past or present Jews in it, she would express first total surprise, and then just a bit of hostility. Like, "Who the hell are you to ask a question like that?" The fact is that the woman who converted probably has forgotten that she's Jewish.

Despite all of the planning and the years of worry

about the wedding, sometimes the thing can become un-tracked. And then the wedding is canceled. When a wedding is canceled, either the bride's mother or the bridegroom's mother has a nervous breakdown. Usually, they both have nervous breakdowns. A nervous breakdown, Italian style, is not like a nervous breakdown in other societies. Nobody is carted away to Bellevue. In our neighborhood, the mother went crazy in the confines of her home amidst the assorted craziness of her family.

One of my mother's cousins recently went through a cancellation, after her daughter's wedding had been in the works for two years. The neighborhood doctor visited her, and as in the case of all nervous breakdowns he pre-scribed a mysterious green medicine. All I know is that from the moment the announcement goes out saying that the marriage of so-and-so will not take place as scheduled, it's chaos. In the case of my mother's cousin, her daughter was twenty-five and so was the guy; they were two old people by neighborhood standards. What drove the cousin to her nervous breakdown was their ages; she didn't think her daughter would ever go through the courtship stage again.

Interesting about Italian nervous breakdowns caused by disrupted wedding plans — most of them last three days. No more, rarely less. The doctor usually makes two house calls a day during the crisis, and by the second day the mother of the bride is so sedated out of her head that *she* thinks the marriage already has been held.

The mourning following a marriage-to-be that has broken up is quite similar to the mourning of a death in the neighborhood. Tears flow, people are crying out loud and striking out blindly at furniture and walls in frustration.

Not only does the immediate family suffer during one of these crises, but *the* aunt usually goes into cardiac arrest and sometimes doesn't pull through. *The* aunt, as opposed to all of the other aunts, is usually the oldest and most venerated relative at a wedding. Her face is lined like a road map and usually in her conversation she thinks she still is living in Naples. A guy can have twelve aunts, but there is always *the* aunt. Most often she can't walk, so during the wedding she holds court and the entire family pays homage to her.

The only other person who is accorded the obeisance of *the* aunt is the uncle who is connected. Mafia. If he isn't the richest guy there, he sure as hell makes out that he is. Everyone pays court to him, just the way they cater to *the* aunt.

Although the causes that wreck a wedding before it takes place are fairly random, one of the things that happens is that a normal prewedding fight over who sits where and next to whom gets bigger and nastier until finally the bride says to the bridegroom, "Forget it. If we can't settle things at this stage of life we're doomed." These fights are also fed by bad cases of nerves. I recall a friend of mine named Ernie whose wedding almost blew apart because the bride-to-be wanted to seat his crazy Uncle Eddy near the band, and my friend's Uncle Eddy hated loud music. Ernie knew that Uncle Eddy was a pain in the ass but Uncle Eddy had been a great help to the family during hard times and Ernie felt that he had an obligation. They compromised by sitting Uncle Eddy next to the girl's deaf aunt and thus saved the whole proceeding.

Hostility between the bride's side and the bridegroom's side is pretty traditional and it begins the moment the engagement is announced. The family of the guy goes over to meet the family of the girl, and that evening is tense from the starting gun, which is the girl's proudly displaying her engagement ring. "Show the ring" comes the command and although the families don't exactly take loupes out and screw them into their eyes right then and there, the appraisal is pretty close to that. "A very nice blue-white diamond," someone might whisper, and inevitably there is a very heavy discussion about the number of carats in relation to other diamonds given recently in the neighborhood.

In many respects the ring is nothing but a source of grief for all concerned. If it's *too* big a ring, then the guy is a show-off; too small, he's a cheapo. The ring is a no-win situation. And since every ring was bought on Forty-seventh Street in Manhattan's diamond district, the cost can't be kept too quiet.

The period from the engagement until the wedding itself is one of delayed, but breathless, anticipation. For two years or so, the collective families are praying that the engagement will not fall apart. About six weeks before the wedding the shower is held.

In Brooklyn, the Chinese have made a fortune out of bridal showers. For some reason unknown to me, showers are always held in Chinese restaurants on Saturday nights. They're supposed to be surprises. When the bride-to-be sits down at a booth with a single friend who has lured her to the restaurant, the entire mob bursts out of the kitchen yelling "Surprise!" and scaring the hell out of the coolies, the patrons, and the bride.

As to gifts, the weird aunt always brings something off-color; well, dirty. In my time it used to be a pack of condoms. Today, of course, we're much more sophisticated — dildoes from exotic Manhattan sex stores. The mother of the bride — who hasn't talked to her own sister for about twenty years — is absolutely wild with anger at the aunt who thinks the whole thing is very funny. The bride is mortified. There always is at least one tasteless gift at every shower. And there are usually two or three toasters.

From then on, it's downhill. The wedding goes off, hopefully without a hitch. In my day the wedding couple always went down to the Sherry Frontenac Hotel in Miami. Today, it's Puerto Rico. The trauma that is Italian marriage begins on the honeymoon. I've got a cousin on my mother's side who put on forty pounds during her honeymoon and now weighs about two hundred and fifty pounds. Her mother still says, "Gee, Rose has a terrible gland problem." My feeling is that Italians must have gland problems unlike any other group of people.

The cycle keeps repeating itself. It's true that now couples don't settle down and then spend the next fifty years of their life in the neighborhood. They get a three-room apartment right down the street from one of the mothers but they start to move out after five or ten years — New Jersey, Staten Island, Long Island. But the patterns don't change. The reverence toward the wedding won't change. The day you see a couple living together for a few years to "try out" the notion of whether they'll get along is unheard of in our society. I casually mentioned this to one of my aunts the other day, saying that this was what some of the more advanced young people were doing in places like New York. Her answer was simple and to the point: "Those communists will do anything. They don't believe in God."

There were two churches in
the neighborhood — Our Lady of Grace R.C. and St.
Simon of Jude R.C. Everyone in the neighborhood went
to one or the other. The Church was probably the single
most damaging force in the neighborhood when I was
growing up. It had the most influence on the neighborhood,
next to the Mafia. The Church had tremendous power, both
hidden and real, and sometimes it had the children for
seven years, then ten years, and finally forever. If the
Church in Spain, Portugal, or Italy ever saw how it was
run in Brooklyn, U.S.A., eyes would have popped. There
was a psychological sophistication that the Church had in
my day — to the degree that, even now when I look back,
I wonder if it could have been so smart. But it was, and
the appeals and how they were phrased were brilliantly
handled.

Essentially, the Church pushed bigotry. If you wanted God you could find Him at Our Lady of Grace or St. Simon of Jude but nowhere else. There was a Protestant church hidden away in our neighborhood. We simply called it the "crazy church," because our neighborhood could not conceive of people living among us not being Catholic. If they weren't Catholic, they were crazy; hence, the "crazy church." The word in the neighborhood was that they did a lot of rolling around the floor in religious ecstasy.

In my family, as in many families, there was no long-standing tradition about which church you "belonged to." That was a concept fostered by other religions. If a house was within one or two blocks of Our Lady of Grace, the people "went" to Our Lady of Grace. And if someone lived near St. Simon of Jude, that's where he went. Either church represented at most a seven- or eight-block walk. There weren't any major differences between the churches; same machinery, same faces, same story to tell.

In my family the church we went to depended on the weather. If it was cold out, someone would say, "It's lousy weather, let's not walk the extra blocks to Our Lady of Grace." So we would pray at St. Simon of Jude. However, there were a couple of good bakeries near one church, and maybe we felt like some fresh rolls or Danish pastry. In that case, we'd say, "I'll go to Our Lady of Grace today because I can hit the bakery after church." Some of the parishioners at Our Lady of Grace, in acknowledging the bakery on Avenue X, said flat out, "We go to Our Lady of Grace because of the bakery."

Picking a church was pretty much a matter of whim. When I say that there were no major differences, I am totally correct. However, I have to admit that Our Lady of Grace always cried poorer than St. Simon of Jude. Even though the entire neighborhood was at the poverty level, Our Lady of Grace was able to convince the people who attended services that they ought to feel guilty. Everyone said that St. Simon of Jude was richer, but who's to know the truth? They never were as *loud* about how poor they were as Our Lady of Grace.

The priest in charge of Our Lady of Grace, Father Taliaferro, was a terrible old man whom I hated from the day I stood behind him in a two-dollar win ticket line at the Jamaica racetrack and saw him cashing in a bundle of tickets on a horse. From then on I never believed his sermons about poverty at Our Lady of Grace.

The guy who ran St. Simon of Jude was named Father Antonioni and he was a very curious fellow. He was tall, wore glasses, and was nervous as hell. Before coming to St. Simon of Jude he had been the priest at Sing Sing prison. I often wondered if he ever looked back on his career and wondered why some priests ended up in St. Patrick's Cathedral in Manhattan, and he was promoted from seminary to Sing Sing to the backwaters of Brooklyn.

Father Antonioni actually moved to our neighborhood without any transitional problems and that's probably because he kept a lot of his old parishioners. He was constantly talking about prisoners who were walking the last mile and how they were always calling out for God. It was very effective stuff and it scared most of the kids out of their wits. "And I was there at the last mile and when they were screaming for their mothers and for God, God could not help them. God was not ready to help them because they had sinned." He brought us right into the room where they electrocuted prisoners and he was particularly good on burning flesh and screams. In Father Antonioni's world they never called the governor for last-minute clemency, or asked for a special last meal. Only for Father Antonioni's particular brand of God.

One of the reasons that St. Simon of Jude was slightly richer was its school — grades one through eight — which gave it quite a marketing edge in the neighborhood.

To combat St. Simon of Jude's school advantage, Our Lady of Grace was constantly conducting building drives. When I pass Our Lady of Grace today, I am stunned by the odd way the parish buildings are matched. There's no particular overall scheme in mind; buildings were put up not according to plan, but after building drives.

Although the two churches were out there competing for the same dollar, I always liked to think that on a quiet Sunday night Father Antonioni would sit down and have a couple of drinks with Father Taliaferro and talk about what kind of attendance and offering they had had that day.

There were no sermons to speak of. These were the salad days of 1947, 1948, and into the early 1950s, the days of that hero of the Church, Senator Joseph McCarthy. McCarthyism was on its way and if we didn't heed the message, Godless Russia was going to swallow us up. Every Sunday we said a prayer for the conversion of Russia. I often wondered if somewhere lost in the wilds of Russia there was a little kid praying for the conversion of the United States.

The priest was constantly sending out letters about atheists, communists, Godless atheists, Godless communists, and occasionally a socialist, although nobody could figure out the distinction.

A lot of the guys praying for the conversion of the

Russians were also praying for the conversion of the extra point after a touchdown to make the spread, so the prayer wasn't too tough a thing to handle. They'd be going down an entire list of conversions — Notre Dame, Southern California, Pitt, and so on — and they'd simply sneak in the Russians someplace between Auburn and Georgia Tech. Look at it another way: the priest is saying that if the Russians don't convert they're going to kill me, but if Penn State doesn't convert the bookie is going to hurt me and *then* he's going to kill me.

For all I know, the priests included Auburn right in their public prayers, because the priests were very much into gambling. They were as knowledgeable about gambling as their parishioners because of the frequent church fairs and bazaars held during the year. Gambling was woven into the fabric of the neighborhood, and the Church wisely used gambling as a way to reach and raise money from the neighborhood. If the Mafia succeeded in the neighborhood through intimidation, then the Church took its signal from the Mafia and tried intimidation to coerce the parish.

Each church would hold at least four bazaars a year, which meant a good eight weekends of out-and-out gambling for the neighborhood under the auspices of the Church. The bazaars were usually held in the auditoriums next to the churches and literally thousands of people attended each one. Ostensibly, each bazaar was keyed to a specific purpose: a building drive, a new wing for the school, a new residence for the monsignor. But that was so much nonsense. Bazaars were held as often as possible just to raise money. The avowed purpose of the bazaar was to give the thing some semblance of respectability.

The main gambling device at the bazaars was the spinning wheel, and men who literally had not one spare dollar would drop five, ten, even twenty dollars on those spinning wheels. Yes, there were prizes. All donated — some willingly, some not so willingly — from the worthy merchants of Avenue U.

Weeks before the bazaar, there would be a cardboard sign in every window up and down Avenue U announcing the forthcoming event. Before each mass there would be a hard-sell announcement about the bazaar; at the ladies' auxiliary meetings there would be talk of the bazaar.

Bazaars were not gluttonous two-week feasts, à la the Neapolitans of Mulberry Street who put on the Festival of San Gennaro, which is the darling of the New York media and features food of every variety for sale. Our bazaars started on a Thursday, usually about three o'clock in the afternoon, and then ran on to Sunday, which was the biggest day of them all. There wasn't any food; maybe soft drinks, but that was about it. Our bazaars were strictly utilitarian — take the money and run. Starting time was set in the afternoon in the hope of snaring kids after they got out of school. Then, the working crowd would start coming in to take a few plays at the wheels from six to seven o'clock. From seven to eight the entire neighborhood ate dinner, and then back to the bazaar from eight until closing time, which might be around eleven. The priests weren't dumb; they knew that in those tedious lives there was little entertainment. No television in those days. And so the bazaars served a purpose. The same kids who were skidding around the floors of the halls during the weddings were also present during the bazaars, again skidding along on the floors.

Since this was a neighborhood born to losing, no one would ever display any emotion when dropping ten or twenty dollars, which very well could have been food money or milk money for the next week. After all, it was for a good cause, wasn't it? The Church *knew* that no one ever showed any emotion when losing, because that was the sign of a real guy.

Although it may have been that when the bazaars first began they truly did have a specific building or project in mind, I imagine that after a while the priests said, The hell with it, let's not tell them why we're doing it, let's just tell them it's happening. And they'll show up.

The scheduling of the bazaars and the various other fund-raisers was a complicated business, because the neighborhood also had its feasts, honoring various saints. We were a tremendous neighborhood for saints. We would drop to our knees and pray to the appropriate saint whenever we thought we needed the slightest help. Eye infection? Give a whistle to Saint Lucy, patron saint for eyes.

Everything connected with the saints was big business. Not only was there gambling, but there was an enormous traffic in religious articles, medals, Bibles, artifacts of all sorts, crosses of all kinds. For example, at every house in the neighborhood there was an enormous statue of the Infant of Prague. I don't know who the Infant of Prague is; I am weak on religious education, but I was strong on knowing what the Infant of Prague looked like (he was blond).

My home, which by no means was a retreat for the devout, still had its share of artifacts. We had saints all over the place, here a statue, there a painting. And plenty of crosses, including a giant job hanging in my parents' bedroom. All the kids wore crosses around their necks. I had a particularly heavy cross around my neck and I discovered that I did not have good feelings about religion. I had been running on the beach and the cross bounced up from my chest, hit me in the mouth, and chipped my tooth. That was the first time I realized that God wasn't really being good to me. And there was no reason why I should be good to Him.

The only civilian (as opposed to a member of the cloth) who made out in the religious department was a guy named Fantelli, who opened a store in the neighborhood dealing strictly in religious articles. He did a landslide business.

The major difference between the feasts and the bazaars — at least in my opinion — was the difference in the way money was raised. In bazaars, the priests were satisfied to put up their wheels and collect at the house odds. But when a feast was about to hit the neighborhood, the priests went through the neighborhood collecting money door to door. This took nerve and guts, because there was always a certain undercurrent of hostility toward the Church, and for the priests to expose their flanks in collecting door to door was a pretty risky business. "I'd like to come in and talk to you" was the way they'd open the conversation after they caught us at home. And what they had to talk about was the upcoming feast and what our contribution was to be.

One of the major feasts was always held in July, when it was broiling. The neighborhood gave thanks that it didn't rain during the feast and the reason it didn't rain was because God had looked down favorably upon the feast. Forget that there had been a twenty-five-day heat wave and not one drop of rain had fallen on the entire Eastern seaboard in a month.

The turnouts for the feasts, like the crowds for the bazaars, were always good. In July, the people of our neighborhood were hanging around. They weren't in the Hamptons or even at Coney Island. They were out on Avenue U and one of the reasons they were all there was that the priests had turned everyone out. The food was sensational and the next day the entire neighborhood had dull, roaring stomachs. Brioschi was very big in our neighborhood the day after a feast.

There were similarities between feasts and weddings. At the wedding, a drunken cousin would always stagger up to the band and demand to sing. At July feasts, there always was one woman who began to sing "The Star-Spangled Banner" in an impromptu performance.

There would be a bandstand set up with a couple of mandolin players. They would patiently wait for the woman to finish and then they, the *professionals*, would launch into their number. In our neighborhood the standard instrument was the mandolin. On the other side of Ocean Parkway, all the Jewish kids were playing the saxophone and planning to be Stan Getz. I once had a cousin named Luigi whose specialty was singing at seedy Italian restaurants and passing the hat, and also singing at feasts. His career had begun with strolling from table to table with a mandolin in some restaurant in Little Italy, then advanced to single spots in restaurants and feasts.

Luigi's big song was "Mama," which was the national anthem of the feast, weddings, Avenue U. Most of the neighborhood truly didn't know the words to "The Star-

Spangled Banner," but they sure as hell knew "Mama." "Mama" usually was the finale to the feast, and more often than not, the priests were the ones to give Luigi the word that it was okay to sing the song. They had collected as much as they were going to collect, so Luigi now could close proceedings. The interesting thing about that song was that it allowed Italian men to let loose their emotion. It was all right to cry during the singing of "Mama," we could weep and carry on all we wanted to. All that stoical, repressed emotion about everything else in life could come out during the song. It was not unusual to see the entire crowd at the feast choked up with emotion, tears running down their collective cheeks. Actually, it wasn't so much a song as it was a prayer to the guy's long-departed mother, and how he missed her. It hit the Italians right where they lived — in bed with their mothers.

When I said before that I once *had* a cousin named Luigi, the reason I put it that way is that the family has not seen Luigi in a very long time. Luigi was the first member of the family to fly on an airplane, jet or otherwise. He came home one day with a worried look on his face and said something about having to get to Florida very fast. Not only did he sing from table to table but he also was a bit of a con man, which may have had something to do with his rapid exit from New York. He also was the first member of the family to have extradition papers drawn against him by the State of New York.

Although the priests from both churches were very visible, high-profile kind of guys, they deliberately did not mingle in the neighborhood. None of that Barry Fitzgerald–Bing Crosby *Going My Way* crap for them. They stayed away from the community. They didn't show up for a Sunday night dinner; they weren't around having delicate cups of tea with their parishioners, because for openers their parishioners were not into tea — they were drinking red wine morning, noon, and night. My feeling is that if the priests hadn't gone into religion, they would have been running some Wall Street bucket-shop hustle. They knew that to mingle would be to weaken their grip on us. They didn't want to be one of the boys; they had to be aloof and a bit mysterious if they expected us to react to them the way they wanted. Contribute, they said. We gave. Pray, they said, or you'll burn in hell. We prayed.

The priests cleverly tied everything in daily life to religion. "Yes, the feast or the bazaar was successful — we can thank God for that. It was God's will." God's will was impressed on all of us — young and old — to such an extent that if the lights went out it was God's will. Car broke down? God's will, and forget that the heap was about to collapse. If a family went broke, like some neighbors of ours did, and ended up evicted on the street right there with their furniture for everyone to see, it was God's will. It took a lot to be evicted in that neighborhood, and nobody around had a dime to help out the family. The Church simply said that being evicted was God's will and, sorry, they couldn't help out with the bank.

It was also God's will that we attend religious instruction. Religious instruction consisted mostly of more talk about Godless atheism and about the horrors of spilling your seed in masturbation. Yes, of course there must have been much more, but all that remains after decades of trying to wipe out the memory of going to religious instruction on Wednesday afternoon is, "Don't tamper with the seed."

We must have been about eleven or twelve years old when the priests began their talk about seed. They were very big on discussing seed, so much so that you would have thought we were walking gardens. Actually, it took us a little time to figure out that when the priests were discussing seed, they were really talking about sex. "The seed must *always* [italics mine] be used to propagate the faith." Thus, one must not waste the seed. The priests took a clinical interest in how your seeds were handled.

During all of this, the Youngs Rubber Company was trying to make a decent living mass-producing contraceptives, and the priests were saying right up front that if I ever slipped one of Youngs's products on, my fingers were going to turn black and then fall off my hand. Masturbation turned you blind, and intercourse — with the protection of a contraceptive — would get you into hell (without fingers).

Don't for a minute think that the Church didn't check up on its own every once in a while. We were subject to periodic visits from a cadre of shock troops from the Jesuits, who would storm into the parish not unlike the way the Marines took Okinawa. The Jesuits were tough, and the Church sent them in whenever the hierarchy thought that the parishioners were getting too soft. No ifs, ands, or buts about the Jesuits. Eyes blazing, they told us in angry voices never to touch anything below our necks until we got married.

Try to imagine what it was like for young men and women coming into young adulthood — and we matured rapidly in that neighborhood. And our friendly visiting Jesuit tells us that if we have desire for someone of the opposite sex, those feelings are ugly, wrong, evil, and disgusting. We were told about how bad lust in the heart was long before Jimmy Carter discovered it.

Of course the party line was that the express reason to have sex is to produce a child. Otherwise, the sex act is filthy and disgusting. Do not do anything like that because it is dirty. Any girl who does have sex before marriage is dirty. If I were to have sex with someone before getting married the two of us would be *consumed* — literally limb by limb — by disease.

I am not exaggerating. The word "enjoyment" was stricken from the dictionary when it came to sex. No fun involved. Intercourse was strictly for the procreation of another Catholic.

We had no venereal disease in the neighborhood because we rarely strayed outside the neighborhood for sex when we were young. But we certainly did not pay attention to the priests when it came to sex. I would imagine that just about everyone indulged in premarital sex. Kids started going together when they were sixteen, but the law said the girls had to wait until they were eighteen to get married. So they had sex. But it was a double header as far as guilt was concerned. First it was sex-with-guilt feelings because we did not have "respect" for the girl involved. In fact, neither of us had any respect for the other, and without respect we obviously did not enjoy ourselves. Second, that old seed problem. Since we were using contraceptives and wasting seed, we were also violating the dictum no sex without a child nine months later. The Church ruined more marriages than any other single force or institution that I can think of. Psychiatrists' offices are full of people today who cannot enjoy sex, are embarrassed by orgasms, who hate the whole business because of a Jesuit way back then scaring the hell out of them.

One day in our neighborhood, Our Lady of Grace got a new priest to replace Father Taliaferro. Our Lady of Grace did not have a school to push religious instruction; in fact, it did not have a lot of things that St. Simon of Jude did have. The man picked to guide Our Lady of Grace in its running competition against St. Simon of Jude was named Father Bertoletti and he came to us straight from Italy. He could not speak one word of English, and thus we all flocked to his confessional. We could tell which booth contained Father Bertoletti from the line waiting eagerly to bend his noncomprehending ear. The Church was screaming at us that if we did not go to confession it was a mortal sin, and when we had mortal sin on our souls there was no simple way out — we got torched. The priests continually told the story of the youth who had committed sins, had sins on his soul, but he went to confession and cleansed himself as was God's will. On his way home the kid died because he tried to drive the transmission off his 1949 Ford. And, although he died, it was okay; he was on his way to heaven because he had been to confession just minutes before. Imagine, they would say, what it would have been like if that kid had not gone to confession. Eternal hell. No discussion, by the way, of the fact that the kid couldn't turn from Ocean Parkway to the service road at eighty miles an hour without killing himself. That story sent us to confession for the rest of our lives, or maybe to race driver's school.

Both Our Lady of Grace and St. Simon of Jude were superb at taking kids and building up the guilt in them for the first seven years of their lives. At the first confession during their first communion these tiny kids were wandering around my neighborhood mumbling to themselves about whether this or that was a mortal sin or a venial sin. We certainly didn't know good thoughts from bad thoughts, and I have no evidence that the priests in our neighborhood knew the difference either.

The problem with the confession situation and the guilt thing was the rumors that floated around the neighborhood as we got older. I went to a public school — P.S. 95 — rather than the St. Simon of Jude school. The moment I hit P.S. 95 I heard that I was pretty dumb to have decided to go to a public school when I, lucky Catholic, had a chance to go to that hotbed of sex and corruption, the parochial school at St. Simon of Jude. And of course I knew that the girls — to a woman — at St. Simon of Jude were hot stuff and fucked. Along with the Jewish girls.

Very early on, sex became a small religious war. We all ran after the girls at St. Simon of Jude, desperately trying to undress them, and getting nothing but, "If it's that kind of thing you're after, why not try the *Jewish* girls?" which gets us, briefly, into the religious situation.

Up front, let me say that the Italians in my neighborhood were consistent: they were as bigoted about "the Jews" as they were about Protestants and anything or anybody who wasn't Italian Catholic. About the Irish, they were violent. Not so the blacks. For the Italians of my youth the blacks simply didn't exist. We had no maids coming into our neighborhood in the morning and then leaving at night. We had no black laboring class working for the store owners on Avenue U. We didn't see blacks. They were from a foreign country.

The rumor went that the young Jewish girls melted at the touch of generations of Italian lovers. They yearned for suave, Mediterranean-complexioned young men, which we all were. What confused the hell out of us when we were fifteen and sixteen was that Christ had been Jewish, too. And that was a fairly heavy thing for most of us to grasp. We always assumed the Jews had killed Christ. I never heard a priest say Christ had been killed by the Jews. I also never heard a priest come out and say that the Jews had *not* killed Christ, either.

It was a Jewish kid named Tully, whom I went to school with, who told me about Christ and his origins. My response was the simple one of disbelief, ranking right next to my disbelief upon learning that babies could be found in women's stomachs. I did not go running to a priest in horror with the news of Christ's origins; I did not seek solace or reassurance. Nor did I think that my small religious world was coming down around my ears. At that point in my life, I couldn't give a shit. Christ could have been Episcopalian for all I cared. I was ready to give him to the Jews, or to any group that wanted to take him in. Disbelief, yes, in hearing the news. But then, in the context of all the nonsense, lies, misinformation given to me for so long by the Church, I thought about it for a minute and then went on to the next case.

By the time most of us hit fifteen in my neighborhood we just about had had it with the Church. We had grown up being pushed and shoved toward religion. The priest said we must bring our parents to church on Sunday, and if we didn't *they* were going to burn in hell, and we sure would be lonely up there in heaven without our parents who would be sweating it out.

So we competed to drag our parents to church. None of us was able to articulate to our parents the desperate need to get them to church, so we simply begged. I was petrified that my parents were going to burn eternally, and there we stood on Sunday, in a packed church. We sweated like hell in the summer because the bodies were jammed in and the perspiration along with the incense produced a musky odor that made you faint.

The priest conducted the mass in Latin of course. He was assisted by two altar boys, who were masses of pimples. The families that produced the altar boys were deeply religious — I mean they lived and breathed the stuff. In those families the little girls at the age of seven or eight decided that they were going to be nuns and that was that — a future Jennifer Jones was born. The same thing with the boys who decided that they were going to become priests. Kids from these families were into volunteer work, making telephone calls for the Church, handing out pamphlets, attending meetings. The machinery of the Church always unerringly picked out the future priests and nuns; somehow, the network said, "This kid is a comer, grab him." And the Church did. At the age of fifteen, when the rest of the neighborhood was finally getting rid of its acne, those kids — future nuns and priests — would blossom out with a second growth of pimples that was nothing short of fantastic. Not only was the Church bad for your mind, but it wrecked your skin.

The altar boys at St. Simon of Jude and Our Lady of Grace seemed to get their biggest thrill out of giving communion. When I was seven and I had been primed through religious instruction about communion, the first time I took communion I was petrified. I am going to receive the body of Christ, I told myself. All I have to do is open my big mouth and the pimply faced altar boy is going to jam a plate under my mouth and the priest is going to slam a wafer onto my tongue.

"You must not chew the wafer," the priests said. "You are receiving the body of Christ. Let it melt on the roof of your mouth." Here comes the priest. He places the wafer in my mouth and the altar boy shoves a communion plate under my chin in case I decide to embarrass the world and spit the wafer up or fumble it and drop it on the floor. It's supposed to melt, I kept telling myself, it's supposed to melt, and the wafer refused to melt. And I said to myself, Gee, here I am receiving the body of Christ but I can't chew Him. He's supposed to melt in my mouth like an M&M but He's not melting, and what the hell am I going to do? A little later, with the wafer still not melted, I began to get a bit nauseous and then what ran through my mind was this: It doesn't taste very good; in fact, it tastes terrible. What happens if I throw up right here in church? Will Christ become an atheist simply because I threw up on the floor?

The legendary stories about parochial schools are all true. Kids did get the hell beat out of them in school. Nuns did pick up heavy rulers and rap people across the knuckles. Heads were banged against walls. Kids were being pounded in the name of religion. I don't think any father went up to a nun and said, "You can't beat my kid." Or, "You just hit my kid so hard across the face his nose bled." People sacrificed to get their kids into the school. Families were assessed as to the number of kids they had in the school. An uncle of mine, a truck driver, desperately wanted to send his kid to St. Simon of Jude's school and couldn't. No money, and no exceptions made. And if a family then got their kid in they still had to make a donation. To the Church. Not to the school fund.

For those people in the neighborhood who *had* to send their kids to the school, it was a time to panic. Even fifty dollars was an enormous amount to many families. And they didn't know how to fight the situation, or what to do. If they didn't send their children to the Catholic school, they would burn. A lot of guys simply held two jobs to make ends meet.

Finally, when I was sixteen, I packed all organized religion in. My family weren't churchgoers, or especially religious. I just stopped going. I never made any dramatic announcement to my family saying I was quitting. I just did. I felt that the Church was part of a gigantic hoax. I wouldn't say that to my friends, though. It simply was the way I felt inside.

And when guys I used to see after church would sort of duck me, the dialogue would go like this: "I'll meet you at the candy store at twelve o'clock." "I'm going to twelve o'clock mass." "Okay, I'll meet you at one o'clock." Nobody went around saying, "Hey, I gave it up." The Church still had its mumbo-jumbo, its hold on people. Seventeen-year-olds still had enough fear of the unknown in them not to tamper too much.

It didn't take anyone too perceptive to look around at the neighborhood and wonder what the great Church had done. True, the churches — Our Lady of Grace and St. Simon of Jude — had grown in size. Buildings had been erected, but for the physical benefit of the churches.

They took so much from the community and gave nothing back. There wasn't an organized sports program so that some of the kids could go out and play basketball. There wasn't a gymnasium so kids could get off the streets. They didn't start a medical clinic so that the poor people did not have to go to strange hospitals or incompetent doctors. Propagate the faith: those were the key words. Which simply meant, throw us some more bodies. Why the school? The schools were essential so that the priests could teach more kids. More kids meant more converts and more families in the bag. Why have more families in the bag? More money. Why more money? To build another school.

So I stopped. I never had the courage to stand up in the neighborhood and say, "Folks, this thing is a gigantic hoax."

But I saw enough to leave. The priest told us that God would help us. To date God hasn't put in an appearance at Avenue U. It still is as desperate a place today as it was thirty years ago. Interesting, that God never told anyone in the neighborhood to stop working as a laborer and go to night school, take some courses, and perhaps try to learn another way to earn a living. That wasn't in the cards.

The Church wanted — and got — to make the neighborhood totally reliant. Or helpless, depending on your point of view. The priests really did not want my grandmother to learn English. They seemed happier when she was ignorant, to such a degree that she couldn't fill out an alien card without the entire family sitting down, figuring out what the form meant. The Church didn't say, "Listen, we've got a class in something terrific called Civics, and maybe you'll learn a little English and perhaps you can become a citizen." No way.

The Church wanted a little bit of Italy right there in the good old U.S.A., and they got it. Never once did the Church say, "Well, we've raised some money and we're going to start a scholarship program and maybe some of you can go to college and escape this place." That was not the role of the Church. The role of the Church was the status quo. The role of the Church everywhere is the status quo. The role of the Mafia is the status quo. Do not ever think for a moment that the Church and the Mafia are dissimilar organizations. They both peddle narcotics: one simply is physiological, the other psychological. It came as no surprise to anyone living in Brooklyn that when some hoods ripped off the jewels of a church the jewels were returned instantly. And a couple of weeks later two bodies were found in a trunk.

Am I bitter? Most certainly. I would not expect to see a neighborhood ground into dust during the middle of the twentieth century in America by the Church. Yes, neighborhoods disappear through racial strife, economic change, and other factors. But because of the Church? I can't help remembering the remark Kefauver made about the neighborhood being the worst breeding area of crime in the U.S.A. And I wonder why no one connected the Mafia to the Church.

I am not exaggerating. This, from the *New York Times*, detailing the final hours of Carlo Gambino:

They came by the hundreds yesterday to a Brooklyn funeral parlor to pay their last respects to Carlo Gambino who came to this country as a stowaway 55 years ago and became the so-called "boss of bosses." . . . With police cameras recording every visitor to the wake, the mourners mounted the steps into the

Cusimano & Russo funeral home on West Sixth Street at the corner of Avenue T. . . .

A funeral mass for Mr. Gambino, who was 74 years old, will be celebrated tomorrow at 10 A.M. at Our Lady of Grace, 430 Avenue W in Brooklyn.

Our Lady of Grace! Local church makes good!

10

Despite the fact that my neighborhood was permanently blighted and had no real industry to speak of, several areas of commerce could qualify as "industry." Gambling was one; stealing from the docks and then fencing the goods was another; the Church was one of the first multinational industries in our neighborhood. Weddings, of course, and then one of the biggest businesses of all: funerals.

Today, as I drive through the neighborhood, I am staggered by the funeral homes, on practically every corner and especially on the main thoroughfare, Avenue U. In the 1940s, when I was growing up, the undertakers hadn't built their establishments; they were operating out of unpretentious two-story buildings and usually funerals and wakes were conducted in the home. The bodies would be embalmed and then returned to the home, laid out in the living room. For three days the body would lie in state, and if there were sons in the family each son would take his turn sitting up all night with the body.

In those days, the undertakers didn't know much about marking up the prices on caskets. They only knew one thing: grief. And there you couldn't find a more competent group of people in the United States in terms of professional tragedy. Of course, that's all the undertaker had to sell in those days — if he couldn't handle the grief in the house, then his only contribution was the delivery of chairs and the coffin.

The undertaker was more of a choreographer than he was an orchestrator. He had three days to provide for the maximum suffering for the family, the maximum amount of tears, the maximum amount of hysterics after the body had been stared at by everybody for three days, and the mourners passing by the coffin were about ready to drop as well.

Even today, the cast of characters in Italian funerals has remained practically the same. Let us say that a grandfather has passed away at the age of seventy-one or seventy-two. Among the bereaved will be at least two sons, one of whom has a heart condition, probably a murmur. And because there is an astonishing amount of emotion let loose over the three days of an Italian wake and funeral, everyone is looking at the son with the heart murmur, saying, "Well, the carrying on and the screaming is going to get him. He's going to go, too, and then we're really going to have a mess on our hands."

There's always one nephew who is a little flaky, a little dangerous, maybe a little violent. His role is to suddenly go berserk. He can go berserk in two major ways. In the first, he starts punching walls or lamps or literally banging his head against a wall (I once saw a cousin of mine hit a bathroom door and splinter it). All of this is accompanied by wailing, tears, and curses. In the second, the flaky nephew tells the priest to go fuck himself. This is the most interesting type of behavior because *everyone* is worried when this takes place. That is, the son with the heart murmur can suddenly yell, "Oh Madonna! Oh Madonna!" and keel over, but the family really doesn't give a damn about him; they're concerned about the cuckoo who has grabbed the priest around his collar and is proceeding to call him a money-grubbing son-of-a-bitch. This can get the entire family into deep trouble, and when this character starts carrying on they all make a move toward him.

It is also an unwritten rule that everyone at an Italian funeral comes down with a lousy cold. The cold usually gets started with the sisters in the family and they spread it to everyone saying, "It's not my fault. Our resistance is low because of the *tragedia.*" So everyone — man, woman, and child — is sniffling and sneezing and running from the nose.

Just as it is predictable that everyone comes down with a cold, it's also written that the women put on black for the funeral — but *everything,* from stockings to dresses to sweaters, is black — and in many cases the black dresses stay with them for the rest of their lives. If the widow is over thirty-five, she puts on black and never removes it again. Ever. I must have been seventeen years old before I realized that the black dress and the slightly sagging black stockings were a uniform of the neighborhood. Now, the woman wearing that black dress started life out wearing a flowered print dress, but at the first funeral she switched to black and that was it.

Actually, it was a four-day holiday, and it knocked off an entire work week. Let's say that the person died on a Monday afternoon. The funeral home would come and take the body away, then return it — probably on Tuesday morning. Then three days of wake would follow, and the funeral itself would be on a Friday.

"When my Joey died . . . ," a lady in black might say. "My Joey" might have been dead for three months, three years, or thirty years. Mourning was a way of life, and when a woman talked about an incident that occurred in 1923, she discussed it as if it took place the day before yesterday.

There's always a group of relatives — aunts, uncles, second cousins, nephews — whose assignment is to be cluckers. A cluck is not exactly like a *tsk, tsk*, but it's close enough; in a way, it's a *tsk, tsk* with fuller body and flavor. "Angelo was such a good person," someone will mutter under his breath, and this is followed by a chorus of clucks, almost like a chicken convention. If a son or a daughter of the deceased breaks down during the three-day mourning period right in full view of the other mourners, a cloud of clucks rises swiftly in the living room. Closely related to the cluckers are the people who don't cluck but make a weird noise by pulling in the sides of their mouths and then issuing a horrendous sucking sound.

No matter how humble the family, or how tough things are financially, there's always a large funeral wreath outside the home of the deceased. Depending on the weather, a knot of people will usually be outside the house during the three days of mourning.

Inside the house, there is a predictable pattern. The body has been returned by the funeral home in its coffin. The first of the mourners, who have been hanging around outside, enter and pay their respects to the family. It is at this particular point that everyone, including those immediately related to the deceased, is overjoyed about "how good he looks." Everyone assures the widow that Rocco looks sensational, in fact "he never looked better. He looks so good that he could get up and walk out of here. Look at him! He's got a glow to his cheeks and" — get this line — "they really didn't have to do much work on him, he's smiling."

The joy in the entire house over how "he" looks is almost contagious. Even the closest relatives — sons, daughters — seem to be elated and there is an enormous amount of talk about the "job." Nobody spells out that the "job" consists of the miracles the undertakers have wrought on one of the meanest looking sons-of-bitches in the world.

Often these are guys who go through life like zombies, and have about as much animation to them as a zucchini, but apparently after a session with the funeral home they're as smiling and fun-filled as the next person.

In the structure of an Italian funeral, the immediate neighbor plays an important role. Often he is the first off the street and into the living room to view the body. His word is the first notice the corpse gets.

In all of this looking at the corpse, all of this evaluation, studying, and general discussing of the deceased almost as if he (or she) were alive and well, there never, absolutely never, is any talk whatsoever about *how* the person came to be dead. In our neighborhood we had any number of people who died early and in their prime, who died suddenly and mysteriously, who died in strange and foreign territories (bottoms of canals, etc.), and who died, as the saying goes, with their boots on. No one ever, I swear, ever said anything other than, "Wasn't it nice that Joe had a smile on his face?" The rule of thumb was: he died of a heart attack. Now it could be that the reason for the heart attack was three bullets in that heart, but we didn't talk about the bullets: only about the fact that the heart stopped ticking. Knifing? The heart just stopped. Dead in mysterious ports such as Ossining or Elmira? Heart. Run down, ice-picked, hung from meat hooks — the heart just quit. And ours was a violent neighborhood where bodies did get discovered, where people were shot; this was not fun-loving Park Avenue. If someone in the neighborhood was in jail, the Avenue U euphemism was "he's away." And if he died violently, "he just died."

If there was a certain morbid status in being the first outsider to view the body, there was infinitely more prestige in having heard the death rattle. One of the things we talked about outside the house of the deceased (when we ran out of comments on how the corpse looked) was the death rattle — how long, how noisy, and so on. As I gather (never having heard a death rattle at first hand), the death rattle is the grinding, peculiar sound a person *in extremis* makes just as he dies.

Quality of death rattles was always discussed because, since almost everyone was dying at home, we took note of little things such as death rattles. And the news of a significant or long-drawn-out death rattle traveled quickly. The first time I realized I was listening to a big discussion about death rattles I simply threw up. But, after that first shock, I got used to it and now — and then — I could discuss the gargle of the rattle with the best of them.

I don't mean to prolong this unnecessarily, but another area of discussion is who closed the eyes after the deceased became deceased. If by chance a doctor happened to be there at the death and the doctor shut the eyelids, that was no good. It only counted if a member of the family shut the eyes; preferably the eldest son.

As soon as the body was displayed and the mourners entered the house to make their condolence calls, they had a big decision to make: to kiss or not to kiss. Were they going to lean over the coffin and give the corpse a kiss on the neck (where else?) or the lips, or were they going to pass that treat by and touch a little flesh — possibly a clammy hand? On my part, there was no decision. Don't touch or kiss anything that isn't moving. With everyone else, though, they really had to do something. And, actually, they usually ended up kissing the lips of the deceased.

Certainly times have changed a bit, because there isn't the emphasis on funerals that there used to be. In the 1940s and 1950s funerals were the Knicks and the Rangers all rolled into one. Along with Christmas and New Year's, death rated as a legal holiday for the Italians.

As with everything else that happens in our lives, we're judged on our attendance. If we filled the seats, we had a good life. After all, death is, in many ways, a terrific spectator sport. The biggest funeral I ever attended took place in the Bay Fiftieth Street area. A distant relative on my wife's side had died. My wife has a large family; that, plus some of his business connections, made for a gigantic turnout. Hundreds of people showed up at the home of the family. Mourners were turned away at the door, and the cops had to come to handle the traffic. My guess is they drew something like eight or nine hundred people in the four days of mourning.

When my grandfather died we didn't have much of a crowd. The family was kind of small on his side. I'd estimate that my grandfather had about two hundred people in the four days, but that's not much of a turnout because a lot of the two hundred were repeats.

My grandfather led a long and honorable life and he died a natural death. The lack of a crowd we had had something to do with this. A lot of the neighborhood attended funerals on a random basis. People showed up who were not related. Indeed, many people did not have any close connection with the family. When a very heavy hitter died under strange circumstances, a hell of a lot of mourners arrived, looking long in the mouth but soaking up every bit of the proceedings. Even today, I have an Aunt Sally who casually attends wakes for people she doesn't know. Or maybe met once or twice in her life at the grocery store.

Attendance was taken at wakes by asking visitors to sign the book as they entered the house. The neighbors living on either side of the deceased usually cooked for the family, but it was simple food. There were very few floral tributes. People did bring mass cards. You could buy a mass card at the church for five dollars or less. The mass cards gave the wake and the funeral a nice sense of the religious, which was something usually missing. A mourner could miss signing the attendance book, but if he gave a mass card his attendance was noted by the family.

One of the first things a family had to do when someone passed away was to go out and buy clothes for the deceased.

Let's face it: here was a man who never wore a tie in his life. Suddenly he's about to wear his first tie, except he's dead. There also were a lot of dead guys in Brooklyn who wore their first suits and white shirts at their own wakes.

The women had been wearing black dresses all of their lives and suddenly, after dying, they ended up wearing powder blue, a color, incidentally, that they wouldn't have been caught dead in if they were alive. And if it wasn't powder blue, it was light pink. Looking at it another way, they were resurrection and/or Easter colors.

For the most part very few people actually displayed the kind of emotions associated with Italians: laughing, screaming, crying, dancing in the streets. This business of Italians wearing their hearts on their sleeves is nonsense. The atmosphere in the parlor or living room where the body was displayed was subdued and, as I said, awkward. No one ever raised his voice; mumbling was the general rule.

It was OK for a member of the immediate family to pull something crazy as hell; that was expected. But how about the guy who isn't immediate family but has to say he's sorry to the relatives and doesn't know how to do that? He's never said "I love you" to anyone before in his life; he's never expressed emotion to anyone before. What's he going to do?

I was raised on mumbling funerals, and until the age of twenty I never knew that any other kind of funeral existed until I had to attend a funeral at Frank Campbell's Funeral Home in Manhattan. It was a case of culture shock. People were talking about the deceased and the coffin was nowhere in sight.

The toughest part of the entire Frank Campbell funeral

came when I was told that the reason the body wasn't around was because it was going to be cremated. I got a little faint when that was spelled out to me. In Brooklyn, we generally believed that eventually all of us would burn, but not in this world. So there we were, sitting in one room during a funeral service, and somewhere on the premises Frank Campbell's troops were putting the torch to a man named Gus.

The craziest part of it all took place when a barbershop quartet entered the room and the leader pulled out a pitch pipe and started humming. It seemed that Gus had been the charter member of a quartet, and in his memory the quartet was going to sing a few songs. It's odd for a kid from Brooklyn sitting in a Manhattan funeral home listening to "Down by the Old Mill Stream," realizing that somewhere nearby the corpse is being reduced to ashes.

What I missed most of all at Campbell's was the priest hanging around. No sooner did the eyelids fall than word reached the priest. Each night he would arrive at the house of the family to do a prayer, a couple of acts of contrition, three or four "Our Fathers" and then off to the next family.

In every family there are at least three or four members who don't talk to one another and, if the occasion were any other than a funeral, they'd be at one another's throats in a minute. But during mourning the word was, "No trouble. He would have wanted it this way." "He," in life, wouldn't have given a damn what they did, but now that "he" was dead, "he" would have liked them to sit and mumble back and forth.

Mourning was not only intense, but exciting as well. New faces, new situations, logistics to figure out. Neighbors provided food for the family of the deceased. It was always the same food, too: chicken soup, a little pastina, perhaps a sandwich, but rarely anything heavy. The thing about the food was that, aside from the irony that the Italians used chicken soup for the dead and the Jews served it to the sick, the food was way outside the Italian norm. For example, I would never get a sandwich in an Italian household on white bread, but during mourning white bread was always served. There always was coffee to drink but no espresso. I don't know why. And no liquor, no wine, no beer. Unless for medicinal purposes.

There was a lot of cigarette smoking: mourners would arrive, pay their respects to the family, sit in the parlor or the living room with the body for as long as they could stand it, and then back outside to stand and smoke.

All of the mourners were terribly conscious that inside the house was a body and inevitably someone would make reference to the body. "Gee," a casual acquaintance would say, "he was a terrific guy. I remember the day he put his arm around me and said, 'Come here, I want to tell you about a horse I've got going at Yonkers.' "

An amazing thing would take place at mournings. The body would begin to take on characteristics that had nothing whatsoever to do with the way the person was in real life.

Now these were not bad people. Oh, occasionally we had a rotten individual, but mostly they were nonentities. They had not done much during their lives, but suddenly they were as astute as Bernard Baruch, as saintly as the Pope.

The body would also develop a magnificent sense of humor, not unlike that of Bob Hope. "He was full of laughs," the mourners would say admiringly, unable to cite chapter or verse.

The mourners were expected to pay their respects to the

family each day. And this just wasn't a casual breeze in the door, breeze out the door kind of visit. There was an unwritten scale of exactly how long the visits had to be. Up to and including deceased aunts and uncles rated about three hours a visit. Any relative closer than that, I would have to spend the full day. Grandmothers and grandfathers on the wife's side took a couple of hours. In fact, the in-law problem was one that always had to be negotiated with the wife ahead of time. She might be pushing for a particular uncle and the response from her husband probably was, "What do you mean we have to spend five hours a day with that bum? He never spent five hours in his entire life with you." And so it went.

We were a neighborhood of limited vocabularies, limited minds, and definitely limited emotions. That guys had to stand around three hours a day for three days saying, over and over, "Gee, it's a tough world. Poor Angelo. How could a thing like this happen?" was a travesty. How could it happen? Well, how about Angelo was seventy-eight years old and had been smoking those vile little black Italian cigars since he was eight years old? That's one reason it might have happened.

The real mourners, the professionals of the neighborhood, knew that the entire week was a staggering drain on the physical and emotional system and they knew how to pace themselves. That first day of intensity and excitement had passed and everyone was settling in for the long haul. Tuesday actually was kind of boring, and friends and neighbors were cleaning up the details: who was there when the death rattle occurred? did the priest make it for the last rites? did the wife (or husband) faint? — things like that. There was prestige in the community in certain items of knowledge. "Did you hear who died?" are the greatest words in any basic religion of the world, and there was a race in Gravesend to be the first town crier on the block. Then, of course, immediately after "Did you hear who?" came "Oh, the minute I heard he died, I put down everything I was doing and came running to the house."

If Monday was exciting and Tuesday was boring, Wednesday was the start of the trauma. In many cases what went on Wednesday was the start of close relationships (many years later) between people like myself and psychiatrists. On Wednesday the coffin was closed.

Although today the coffin has usually been closed, flanked by a bunch of guys in black suits and enough candles to put Con Ed out of business, the ceremony and the emotion are the same. When I was growing up, the coffin was usually at home, and open.

No matter. The only difference is that at today's funeral home when people start to faint (and they really do), smelling salts are available. In the old days we used to shove a bottle of cheap whiskey under the nose of the stricken to revive him or her. "We are about to close the coffin on this good man for the *very* last time. Anyone wanting to pay *very* last respects must do so now." Catch the emphasis on *very*. That really triggered the wailing.

The idea here is very simple: stretch the emotions to the very last inch and strip away any remaining dignity the family might have had. For the kiddies who had been dragged through this three-day exercise in horror there was one more joy — they were about to be lifted up so they could give waxy-looking Grandpa or Grandma a formaldehyde-smelling kiss. How many people would like to be a frightened five-year-old dangled over a coffin, not knowing whether he was going to be dropped in or not?

The priest, who might have been attending up till now by rote, began to throw some real feeling into the proceedings. As the undertaker was telling everyone to line up for one last look, the priest was leading everyone in one last prayer. There was no urgency to any of this. It was slow, dragged out, even stretched beyond belief to milk the people of that extra tear, that extra scream of pain. They never cut any corners.

The undertakers were masters at this. They were able to destroy the nerves of the living for one hell of a long time, if not forever.

Naturally, the funeral homes prospered. The tiny storefront funeral homes of my day grew until today there is as grotesque a collection of huge combination funeral homes/catering halls as can be seen this side of California. There always was a lot of talk in the neighborhood that the reason they prospered was that many of the proprietors were associated with certain business organizations that were not quite the Rotary or the Kiwanis. And, further, there were other stories about rather unusual burials. Such as: very respectable citizens being buried on top of the last remains of a torpedo from the Profaci Family. This was known politely as a double decker.

But the undertakers didn't need double billing, as it were, to get ahead. There was enough business without any fooling around. Even those undertakers who weren't so diligent made out terrifically. I used to have a friend named Eddy who worked for an undertaker. He was a driver when I knew him, and his main function was to pick up the bodies after the funeral and take them to the cemetery in Queens. To get from Brooklyn to Queens Eddy used a pickup truck. The cemetery was near a racetrack (the old Aqueduct) and Eddy sometimes had a problem.

Eddy would pick up the body and try like hell to catch a few races at Aqueduct. Between races, when he should have been reading the racing form, he'd have to dash out to the parking lot just to check up on the body. He didn't do too well at the track on those days when he had the pickup truck with him, because he was always worrying what would happen if some kid decided to steal the truck.

Although Eddy's reputation in the neighborhood as an undertaker was in direct proportion to his ability as a horseplayer, most of the undertakers were respected members of the community.

If the undertakers had been clever about playing on the emotions of the family when the body was at home, well, they were rank amateurs when compared to what the priests and the Church were about to do.

The most traumatic and scary funeral *I* ever attended happened to be that of my grandmother, who died fifteen years ago. My brother and I were standing outside the church on a cold, snowy day waiting to go into the church, and I realized that I hadn't been inside any church of any denomination for some fifteen years. I was completely out of it. I said to my brother, "I wonder what it's going to be like, walking back into a church?" He shrugged. Someone gave the signal for the bells to start tolling, and we started up the steps to the church. Just as we reached the entrance of the church, the reverberations of the bells, or something, dislodged a daggerlike piece of ice. The piece of ice fell some two stories and cracked me on the back of my neck as I was about to take my first step into church.

The impact knocked me to the ground and I was pierced and bleeding. There I lay, at the door of the church, stunned like an ox, with a smear of symbolic blood on my neck, my entire family staring at me, and the only thing I could say to my brother was, "Well, I guess things have changed. It used to be He would throw lightning bolts at you. Now He's tossing snowballs." And with that my brother and I started laughing hysterically, as the priests tried to get us into the church and start the service.

After the church service the coffin leaves in the hands of six professional and bored-looking pallbearers, and then it's on to Queens and the cemetery. This is the moment we've all been waiting for.

The immediate party are given roses by the undertaker, who is making sure to extract that last tear. As the casket sinks slowly into the good earth of Queens, the family members are supposed to toss the roses in the grave.

If there were a lot of emotions sprayed around up till now, the cemetery is the spot where people can really get hurt.

Ci vado io in Italian means, literally, "I'm going there." At a clammy cemetery in Queens, New York, it means a sudden malady that grips the assemblage. Translated even further, it adds up to "Take me instead." The old substitution theory. Maybe one of these days at an Italian funeral God *is* going to take that person up on his offer and bring the corpse back to life. Then we'll see how many people casually offer themselves instead of the deceased. This sudden urge to jump into the grave is not particularly original or ethnic or peculiar to the Italians. But at the Italian funeral the family in the front line *knows* someone is going to jump into the grave. Someone always does. It is my contention that at every Italian funeral, no matter if in this country, Italy, or even among the Italian community in Istanbul, someone will always take a stab at jumping. It is in our blood. We lose at wars, but we sure as hell know how to jump into graves.

Mind you, this old lady of sixty who finally is putting her husband away, much to everyone's relief, is looking forward to just sleeping for another twenty years. But she's also saying to herself, "I'm going to take a jump, just for Vito's sake."

But Mama's two sons (or her two nephews, or her two grandsons, or whatever) whisper to one another, "You stand on one side, I'll take the other." The guy with the heart murmur is told to stand aside, nothing is going to happen. A healthy relative is always assigned to keep an eye on him, but it's a token assignment because if he really does keel over it couldn't have been prevented and it is going to be real trouble. It's almost like the Secret Service, with guys scanning the crowd looking for trouble. In this case, family members are looking for jumpers.

The priest, of course, is doing his best to drive everyone into the grave. This is the priest's last shot at producing tears and he knows *his* reputation depends on the results: "He's going into the earth for the last time, where he never will be seen again by anyone." Translation: "Listen folks, I know, and you know, that this guy was an unmitigated bum all his life, but if you don't carry on now you'll feel guilty for the rest of your lives. Last offer for tears."

Occasionally an aunt goes bats and tries a jump, but usually it's the wife. To uphold tradition. She always looks from side to side, warning everyone as she starts to go.

She gets two steps — no more — and as she begins to pitch forward the sons swoop her up, saying, "Ma, he wouldn't want it this way" (translation: "First he died, and now you're going to break a leg over the schmuck?") or, "Look at poor Willie with the lousy heart murmur. If you jump, Willie is going to die of shock" (translation: "We got enough on our hands, Ma, for God's sake knock it off").

Meanwhile the assemblage is humming at this dramatic interlude; the guys with shovels are looking bored as hell because they've been through this time and again.

The closest to a successful jump I saw was somebody who didn't know how to jump properly and she really scared everyone. Her trunk started forward, ahead of her legs. Thus, she was really on her way down and they just managed to grab her legs. If she had gone, she would have split her lip open on the edge of the coffin as it was being lowered.

The two sons have cleverly inserted smelling salts in each nostril of their mother, and they've dragged her back to one of the cars and stuffed her into the back seat. By now the funeral is winding down.

The roses are tossed in, the grave is filled in, the priest heads for the next funeral, and the crowd splits.

Back at the family's house a light lunch of sandwiches is consumed, and the relatives start to trickle home Thursday afternoon. The widow breathes a sigh of relief and gets ready for twenty-five years of mourning.

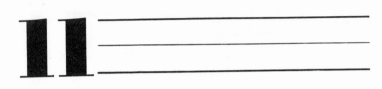

Most of the neighborhood went straight, despite the odds, which in some cases were staggering. When I was sixteen I got picked up by the cops for questioning and then was booked by mistake for drug possession. The cops didn't care if they had confused my name with someone named Gerald, whom they were looking for for pushing heroin. I was lucky. A friend's brother happened to know a lieutenant and managed to get the Jerry–Gerald problem straightened out, but it doesn't take too much imagination to see how one mistake can lead to another.

About three months ago my wife and I were invited to two parties, one in Connecticut, the other in New Rochelle. Essentially, they were reunion parties.

The first party was held in Stamford and was thrown by a close friend of mine named Al. He works for a software company and he sells whatever software companies sell to people who own all of the computer hardware. I guess I went to both of the parties out of morbid curiosity. In a way it was like every bad war movie you've ever seen: after the conflict the survivors of the platoon (Richard Conte, Telly Savalas, Robert Strauss, George Peppard, and Harvey Lembeck) all get together for dinner and see what they each look like now that it's all over. We survived the war; how are we surviving the peace? Honestly, I wanted to test my reactions upon viewing the survivors.

It was the first time I'd seen this group in about seven years. There were ten couples, and we had been very close in the neighborhood. In comparison to the rest of the people I grew up with, this was the upper level of the neighborhood — in intelligence and ambition. This party was the *crème de la crème* of West Seventh Street.

Jimmy's house was a standard four-bedroom, two-bath house in one of those fifteen-year-old developments that had been thrown up casually and is now beginning to show its age. The lot was small and the trees were finally taking hold. The first impression I got as I walked through the door was baldness and fat. Everyone in the group had been putting on weight and just about all of the men had lost most of their hair.

The twenty of us sat around talking in a very studied manner for about ten to fifteen minutes and then suddenly, as if by magic, the group separated, almost like a parting of the sea. The men went to one side of the room and stayed there for the rest of the evening; the women went to the other side. When that happened I almost fell down because suddenly we were thrown back to a church dance at Our

Lady of Grace twenty-five years ago and we were still acting the same way.

The talk was predictable and disappointing. The people who lived in similar places in New Jersey and Staten Island talked about the blacks moving in. The guys having trouble with their jobs talked about the Jews cutting off their promotions.

Everyone drank whiskey sours. They looked at me as if I were a freak because I tried to find some white wine to drink. The men talked mostly about baseball. Everyone desperately wanted his kids to grow up and become baseball players. One of our group was unable to make it: Phil Pepe of the *News*. Phil is the idol of us all, the dream of every closet jock. He *knows* real ball players and talks to them on a first-name basis. He goes to literally every game he wants to, and this is still a group that only occasionally goes to a game.

In catching up on small talk, the group realized that I was from the moon so far as they were concerned. I talked about my diet and about losing weight and cholesterol. I also said that I liked to go to restaurants and eat and when I do I don't particularly like my kids around. One of the guys said, "Well, you always were a Jew." Everyone laughed. Now, these people can afford a restaurant — maybe not Lutèce, but they've got the buying power for an occasional night out.

They haven't left the neighborhood, even though they're living up in Stamford; they don't travel, they eat at home, they stay at home, they don't leave the protective coloration of their nests.

The most popular guy in the group, Frankie, has become

an ultraconservative and was a Reagan man through and through. He didn't vote for anyone after that liberal Ford got the nomination. There are no professional men in the group. We have a couple of minor functionaries in a bank. Another fellow is in the garment center. One of the most successful guys owns clothing stores. Our group has never worked in newspapers, magazines, television, advertising, the entire spectrum of mass communication. We've got people in the food business, a couple of firemen and cops, one guy who owns his own garbage truck and is an independent sanitation operator. We've got two people working for the city in minor civil service jobs.

One of the group, named Nick, is a very bright guy and his achievement — employment as an office worker — just isn't anywhere near his capability. He has slowly come to understand this and the frustration of the fact is eating him up inside. He replays his life constantly, wondering where he went off the track and what he could have done differently. He and a few of the others are suddenly understanding that they've been screwed by a terrible system. They've struck out in their own particular Little League.

Another thing is occurring: middle age is beginning to move in on them in painful and cruel ways. One of the cops in the group spent about ten minutes talking about his feet and how they always hurt him. He's forty years old, and when the rest of us listened to his complaints we all made sympathetic noises. The other cop in the group rides a patrol car in one of the worst sections of Brooklyn and spends the entire day trying to comprehend blacks and Puerto Ricans in the slums. He can't understand them and he hates them. "My life is rapping people with my stick," he said, and he can't fathom that he was unable to get out of our old neighborhood, nor did the neighborhood ever leave him.

One of the firemen says plaintively, "I'm starting to get chest pains after dragging a hose from one room to another during a fire." He's constantly calculating how many years to retirement and how much he'll need to make ends meet.

There was a subtle difference in the two parties — the first in Stamford, and the second in New Rochelle. The first bunch might have gone to night school for a couple of years. The difference is so slight that of the twenty people in Stamford, at least eight of them were carryovers in New Rochelle.

Now, there also are the guys with grease under their nails seven days a week. Machinists, mechanics, drill-press operators, longshoremen, teamsters, fishmongers, construction guys — the working men and the true blue collars of the neighborhood. We rarely see them in a social situation. Occasionally I run into them when I'm back in the neighborhood, but they're not at the parties.

The people at Party No. 2 had gained just as much weight as the people at Party No. 1 had. There were three or four guys at each party who had gone all the way up to 250 or 300 pounds; and there were several women at each party who were pushing 200. It was the kind of weight where you knew they weren't thinking of diets, and it wasn't the kind of weight where you look at a person and suggest knocking off ten pounds or so. It was old-age weight that is there to stay.

Their attitudes were old-age, too. The fireman was not the only one looking forward to retirement: it was something obviously on everyone's mind. They talked lovingly about "puttering around." They all seemed to have crazy hobbies. One guy had turned his basement into the most complete miniature car racing circuit in Brooklyn. Several of the men were members of model railroad clubs. A couple played golf, but not seriously, and I really couldn't figure whether anyone did any serious exercise. They all were into spectator sports; no bicycle riding, no tennis, no jogging, no pretense at fitness. They got married and went to hell. And yet when you take a look at some of the worst fatness and say, "Ah, maybe you've gone a bit overboard," they point to their stomachs and say, "That's the good life." They are saying, "I've got a stomach, my wife has a stomach, and what that means is that we've got this whole thing put together and I made it."

If you were to ask that group, "What's a tranquilizer, and do you have to take a little to keep you going?" they'd either play dumb or say they don't take the stuff at all. There's no Valium to be seen. They have no problems, they say, and they make jokes about "shrinks." Categorically, not one of my group has ever — or will in the future — consulted a psychiatrist. When I mentioned to a couple of the guys that I had tried therapy, one of them said, "But you're a Jew." Meaning Jews go to shrinks and use Valium, but *we* don't need it. Fill the stomach and the head will follow.

Both parties were held on Saturday nights because my old neighborhood doesn't know how to go out during the week. Weekdays are for television and hobbies: if you go out, it's on Friday or Saturday night and Sundays, naturally, are for visiting family and relatives — either back at the old neighborhood or in your home. These are very regimented people and they need their eight hours of sleep. An aunt of mine once said to me, "Jerry, if you don't sleep there's something wrong with you." But I never slept as a kid and that makes me different.

Party No. 1 was held at eight o'clock at night, thus no formal sitdown dinner. The guests, however, figuring that they were going to be ready for a snack at some point in the proceedings, brought cakes. So there must have been six or seven cakes, all of which were homemade.

I'm not criticizing my friends, or judging them. I am, however, frustrated by them. They deserved more. We built a wall around ourselves in the neighborhood and when we built that wall we realized that nobody could get in but we didn't perceive that nobody could get out. The wall is in New Jersey now, and in New Rochelle, and in Staten Island, too. We simply picked the damned thing up and carried it with us. The group still talks about the Jews the way they used to, not realizing that this anti-Semitism is killing them, but now they've got added starters, blacks and Puerto Ricans, who are coming up fast on the outside.

Although they wrongly perceive "the Jews" as a problem where the group works, the blacks are a threat to property values where they live. New Rochelle has a tension in the air and there are racial problems. Al, the host, is talking frantically about the quality of the schools in Connecticut (this from a guy who had to be driven to school with a gun at his head) and he's worried about "declining property values" on his four-bedroom number. Those are magic words to my group — property values — and it's safe to say they would not have known what the hell you were talking about if you'd confronted them with the concept twenty years ago.

While the men are standing around worried about the blacks, the women are talking to each other about their

day-to-day existence. Most of them are very happy with
their lot; they have their houses, they're charged with
taking care of the interior of the house and the kids and the
meals. They wake up in the mornings, they put the kids
through their paces, they start dinner, and then they begin
"cleaning up." The houses are spotless, they gleam, they
are a testament to the huge soap industry of America. The
women are in bed by 11 P.M. The women are a product of
their neighborhood *and* their mothers, which is a hell of a
tough combination.

One of the guys from my group sauntered over to the
women's group and said, "Hi girls, what are you talking
about?" I swear that three of them smiled and said, "Food."
In this respect, you could instantly age them and place
them back on the front sidewalks of those houses on West
Seventh and West Eighth streets, and they're dead ringers
for their grandmothers. In many respects, their lives have
changed even less than their husbands'.

The bottom line for all of the survivors of the neighborhood was expressed by one guy who said, "Man, I stayed
out of jail!" That's a fairly elementary thing to be thankful
for, but it is the overriding thought for many of them.
"Gee, wasn't it crazy in the old days?" said a guy named
Sally (Salvatore). Everyone nodded agreement and the
entire group started talking about the closest thing we have
to a celebrity — the hoodlum Joey Gielli. Gielli anecdotes
were recalled and everyone seemed to have a different story
to tell about him.

All the men from the neighborhood have been mistreated
by time. They had their youth and they married at the age
of nineteen or twenty. Suddenly, at the age of forty, they

became old. They lost their middle age someplace along the line, and it is becoming apparent to them that their lives are just about over with.

They're a group who have spent a lifetime looking at the want ads, whether for used cars or furniture or maybe for a new job. But they really don't leave their jobs unless there is a recession and they happen to get fired. Steady is the word for it. No job-hopping and no experimentation. No changing of occupation at midlife. And, in fact, they wouldn't know a midlife crisis if it hit them in the face.

Although the men were on one side of the room and the women on the other, there was absolutely no talk about sex. I thought that on a Saturday night, emboldened by a few whiskey sours, there might be an off-color joke or two, a description of a fling, but no. Random sex is *verboten;* tattooed on each man's brain are the words, "Thou Shalt Not Fuck Around!" And they don't, not this group. You won't find any deviation in anything these people do. Straight Republican ticket and straight Italian food. Give me Chevrolet and Ford or give me nothing. Anytime anyone suggests something a little unusual — a French restaurant, a Japanese car — he who makes the suggestion is immediately labeled Jewish.

The most staggering fact about the group is that, after twenty years, there is not one single divorce among us. Not one. They are happy, at least on the face of it. There are no sly digs from the women. At a party where some drinking is going on you'll occasionally pick up subtle hints of trauma in a marriage. None of that at the two parties I attended. No wife ever says to her husband, "Why can't you make more money so we can live better and have better things?" I've never heard a wife say, "Why can't we go to something better than a motel at Lake George for two weeks in the summertime?"

The ambitious wife, that cornerstone of American drama, is not around. If anything, the reverse is true: there is a fantastic dependence on the husband, and the wife is saying in effect: "I love him for all his faults. He has provided for me in a better fashion than I had when I was growing up. We have things I only dreamed about as a child (dishwasher, car, detached and private house). It's warm and comfortable in *my* house, the kids are growing up. *Nobody's in trouble. Nobody's in trouble.*"

The national average for divorce is rapidly approaching fifty percent, and yet the specter of same seems to have passed over their heads. What the hell are the odds on twenty people — ten couples — getting married in the years 1957–1958 and not one divorce? What it also means is that their parents began the trend, because God knows the older generation didn't even know what the word meant. I can't believe that there hasn't been a trial separation among my friends. Forget about marriage counselors: they would be regarded as Jewish and not to be trusted. How can it be in that group not one woman has said, "Jesus, I'm going to get rid of that son-of-a-bitch"?

In an earlier chapter I mentioned a fantastic time warp, and the two parties I attended drove that point home. One guy referred to Jews as "Christ killers" and that is a fairly dated piece of bigotry; another called a local Chinese restaurant "Chink's." Forgetting your ethnic sensibilities for a moment, the language is out of synch and from another era. "Jigs" for blacks? It makes no sense. One of the guys remarked casually as we were listening to some old Sinatra records, "They don't make them the way they used to. I love Stan Kenton and June Christy." Voices from the Swinging Fifties.

As far as personal habits go, the gambling has just about gone; the money isn't there. At great personal sacrifice, there are no more horses, crap games. At best there's poker with the neighbors in the finished basement, with the entire scene looking as if it were out of a beer commercial. But the smoking has doubled. Everyone is smoking, men and women, and their consumption seems awfully high to me. Jews gamble, and they also try to cut down on their smoking: I qualified on both scores. As far as dope goes, I will testify that no one in my group has ever done dope, or will ever do dope. Most of my bunch don't really know what cocaine is.

We aren't a minority; there are more people of Italian extraction living in this country than there are blacks, and in that regard we're a majority. If you want to compare us to Poles, Germans, Irish, Chinese, you name it, the Italians have fewer doctors, lawyers, teachers, and professional men than any other ethnic group. And we did it to ourselves. We have plenty of baseball players, boxers, firemen, cops, and storekeepers. My God, we must own the franchise on waiters and cooks. But somehow we don't turn out the people who are going to be on top.

Yes, we produced Sirica, but not Oliver Wendell Holmes, or Warren Burger, or Learned Hand. The Italian Americans got embarrassingly excited when one of ours, Lee Iacocca, became a Ford Motor Company vice president. Yes, the Bank of America, but that's about it. The shame of all this is that we become so damned proud of one Iacocca. It's not a source of pride to me about our representation in national life. Italian Americans don't dominate the media, we're not influential in banking, we sure as hell don't seem to be involved in the creative arts, we seem to have trouble turning out readers and writers, we're not fully represented in Congress in proportion to our population, we're not leading our share of corporations. We do not turn out people who are going to be on top. Except for gin-mill singers, smiling waiters, and twenty or so million people with the ability to point to their stomachs and say, "Hey, life is good to us."

I am utterly convinced that Italian Americans throughout this country began life with all of the equipment needed to get ahead: drive, energy, intelligence. I am also utterly convinced that in every Italian neighborhood throughout this country — Boston's North End, San Francisco's North Beach district — the pressures are murderous on the young from the family to get settled: find a rut and settle in a comfortable manner and stay there. My friends had the I.Q. One of them had an I.Q. of 125 or so and he scrambled for the right to become a cop in New York for the rest of his life. He wasn't meant to be a cop, but some higher deity said, "You have *got* to be a cop." He could not have been a doctor; it wasn't in the roll of the dice. Most Italian Americans most of the time are at the mercy of someone else's whim. They have learned nothing from the pain of growing up — also at the whim of a landlord, the government, the gas company. They sell the insurance fearful they won't make their quotas; they struggle as firemen worried about their health and whether the city of New York will suddenly lop them off the payroll. A man works for a department store and he can look forward to nothing except perhaps another department store. None of my friends had any control over his life and I would have thought someplace along the line they'd have learned a lesson.

Part of it comes from the fact that Italians (forgetting Ethiopia for a moment) are a passive people, almost docile. And my friends and I are Eisenhower's children. The women dress modestly and the men wear weird-colored double knits. They're very straight and when they look at television and see Sammy Davis, Jr., I'll tell you what they see: "a jig who also is a Jew." They don't look their age; they look seven to ten years older. They don't like many people who aren't their own, but if you are one of them — as I am, and I take pride in it — they'll tolerate you to a degree. I'm their Jewish deviate, the man who has obviously gone astray, but then that amuses them.

I have a beard and a completely shaved head and when they saw that combination they nervously said, "Hey, hey, Jerry, you always were a little different." There wasn't another beard at either party, and that goes for mustaches, too. One guy said, "If my kid grows a beard I'll break his legs." And he meant it. To their way of thinking, the finish line was placed at the age of forty and they've made it. Leave us alone. And when a race is over, finish your pasta on the plate, pick up a few calories, and then light up a cigarette.

In certain respects my friends feel sorry for me. "Jesus," said a man named Bobby, "it must be hard as hell having to go with business clients to strange restaurants during the middle of the week." There is real sympathy because I have to be present for duty during the week and then I have to suffer at a foreign restaurant like the Four Seasons. They realize that I have become successful, but it sure as hell isn't on their terms. I have to associate with strange people, eat in weird places, and mingle with friends of the wrong political persuasion. I'm a victim of all the trappings of success. "Well," said one guy, "if you're going to make so much money I guess you got to eat in those French restaurants." And everyone nodded sympathetically.

I'm not sure if *The Summer of '42* is the right comparison. Maybe it's more like *The Best Years of Our Lives*, and truly the best years of their lives were twenty years ago. They loved growing up, it was always safe and warm. And then I mentioned that my wife and I had gone to see *Deep Throat* to try to figure out what the fuss was about. When I said that, there was a shocked silence and one of the women said, "Oh my God!" I started off by grinning and then I realized that I had made a horrendous mistake. My feeling is that if you're still able to achieve an erection at the age of forty, then pornography shouldn't shock you. Maybe wait until you're sixty to be upset, but not forty. The reaction — and I think I'm being fair in summarizing their feelings — was about the same as if I had decided to expose myself. "That's disgusting," one of the men said, "absolutely filthy." Nobody was kidding around about my being Jewish when it came to that remark; this time they knew it for sure. We couldn't have done anything more shocking if we had burned someone at the stake. Nobody in the group had ever attended a porno movie. "It's terrible what's going on in this country," a woman named Carmen said, "just terrible."

I also started a discussion about politics and quickly

learned that everyone was deeply committed to Ford except for one salesman who said, "Fuck Ford. He hasn't done a thing for me. I'm a fucking salesman and the fucking cost of living goes up and up. I'm voting for Carter and if Carter doesn't do anything for the cost of living, fuck Carter." The use of the active verb "fuck" was confined to the men's group. The women wouldn't stand for it.

The question that keeps going through my mind is: what will happen? When in God's name will we change? If ever. My grandmother came here in 1910 and the sense of isolation was there *before* she arrived. The only assimilation is when the men are more concerned with their sons' Little League status. And that's after three generations of the so-called American Experience.

The only salvation, I think, is for the neighborhood as it is now constituted to undergo cataclysmic change — and this may well happen. The Irish are beginning to move in — even on West Seventh Street — and I think in five years or so black families will take a chance at trying to survive. Our mothers are still on Avenue U, but the sons are trying to talk them into moving to the safer shores of Long Island and New Jersey. It's very odd to sit at a party and listen to a balding, pudgy forty-year-old say with great intensity, "I've got to get Mom out soon. The neighborhood is going . . ." You'd think the Germans were marching on Paris or something.

The mothers aren't going to move, I don't think. We're going to have to wait until they die off. Also, there's a new supply of mothers coming in: recent immigrants from Italy go directly to the neighborhood and do not stop first at Mulberry Street. The median age of the neighborhood has gone up. The only people left behind are the very old and those of our group who never married, like some rear-guard holding action in a war movie. Those forty-year-olds are still shooting craps on Sunday and getting drunk on Saturday night.

The young are fleeing. They want a "safe" neighborhood and they cite possible racial changes as a threat to "safety." Forget that in the old days guys were running up and down the streets shooting each other and those guys were a hell of a lot more dangerous than a black family. Nobody gets married and then stays in the neighborhood. They move first to a "better" section of Brooklyn and then the big jump across the river — either New Jersey or Staten Island.

I don't know if the breaking up of my neighborhood will mean more of a life for the children of my friends or not. From the looks of my peers, the Italian isolation is still there and it goes to prove that the potential exists for the Italians to remain the only group that has come to this country and *never* assimilated in the true sense of the word. This is a thought which fills me with despair. Am *I* the freak because I like an occasional French or Japanese meal, have friends who are black or Jewish, now and then converse with a therapist? Perhaps I've been too harsh on my friends, and maybe I really am the odd man out.

But the despair lingers on. Just the other day I happened to be in a fish store in the East Fifties run by a nice Italian fellow named Johnny. He was cleaning a mackerel for me and it was extremely tricky, the fish was very delicate and it needed a deft touch to remove all of the bones. Looking on was the greengrocer from across the street — named Joe. After a while Joe said to Johnny, "You're doing a nice job." And the fishmonger replied, "Well, I ought to. All my life I

wanted to go to medical school. This is the closest I got."
He said it with a straight face, and I still don't know
whether he's kidding or not.

Consider the alternatives. Even if he were making a
small joke, what in God's name can be going on in
Johnny's head even to come up with such a line? What is
his frame of reference marching through life? And if it's
true, then what? Can it be that a failed medical student
ends up owning (in partnership) a fish store on First
Avenue in New York City? And what about his desperation,
his quiet despair? I am sure in the small of the morning
as he tries to sleep he replays his life over and over in the
projection room of his memory, wondering where it went
wrong.

If you work in fish fourteen hours a day, six days a
week, it never leaves you — physically. Johnny is re-
minded of his position every day of the year and by the
time he is forty he will have lost his sunny Italian disposi-
tion. His life will be over and done with and the bitterness
which will overcome his body and his mind will have all
of the sting of a pitch-black cup of coffee, served by a
grinning fool of a waiter who desperately wants to leave
his job in a Naples café and move to the wonderful and
stupendous United States of America, where he has a cousin
living . . . in a place called Brooklyn.

12

Travel may be broadening for most people, but for Italians it's just about the worst thing they can do. The reason is that Italians think and take it for granted that wherever they go the conditions are going to be identical to those they just left. As if being Italian is something universal. Not so; in fact, just the opposite.

Let's take my mother, for example. About five years ago she decided to take a trip back to the promised land — Naples. She and my father had talked about a trip back to the Old Country and now it was time to do it. "Go ahead, Ma," my wife and I said. "It'll be wonderful, fantastic." My parents agreed. After all, my mother had been sitting around in kitchens in Brooklyn for forty years talking about what a paradise she had left to come to New York and now it was time to see how life was really lived. My mother wasn't the only one talking about how terrific it was "back there." All of them did, knocking down wine, complaining about New York, fantasizing about the dancing and the sunshine and the people and the happiness in Naples.

So, off she went. And the very first day — *one day* — the trip blew apart. She took one look at Naples and saw it was a dump. Not only didn't she hear any mandolins playing, she felt very threatened and the first thing she did was take her jewelry, knot it in a handkerchief, and hide it in the bottom of her pocketbook. My father caught the hostility in some of the faces and hid his money in his shoe.

They gave it just one night and then took off. Like many Italians I know, my parents simply couldn't handle it. They headed for Rome and then home — their dream slightly shattered.

My wife and I didn't learn from my parents' experience, and we, too, thought you could go home again. About three years ago we decided to take a look at the home country and my wife and I started out in Milan. The people struck us as very rude, so from Milan we figured we'd stand a better chance in Naples. Although I could handle the language without too much trouble, the city simply seemed dirty, with nothing to do. We ended up in Rome, and if you've seen the Sistine Chapel forty times you can tell yourself it's terrific, but then what? Rome is a big city and the people who live there look down at outsiders. We got into a cab and I figured I'd throw a little Italian at the driver. He turned around and in stone-cold English told me not to speak Italian, please, he could handle English without any trouble. The guy simply put me away and that's the way it was throughout the week we were there.

We didn't like the way a fancy restaurant prepared a pasta dish and were given a pretty rude answer for our trouble. Finally, we said the hell with it and flew to England, where they spoke English without an accent.

Every Italian has trouble going back. The guy from New Jersey who feels he must take a look at the quaint village near Palermo where he grew up — those trips always end up in disaster. I know one fellow from Jersey — Rick — who arrived in Sicily and then started hearing stories about the real Mafia, the outfit where they shoot with shotguns and then ask questions much, much later. Rick suddenly got petrified that the Mafia Mafia was going to kidnap him and demand a ransom, so he hid in his room for nine days and ten nights.

The Italians who have the most trouble are the older ones, those people in their sixties who have been working on a dream in their heads for decades. They're the ones who are the most disappointed when they hit Italy, but even the younger generation — like myself — gets upset when Italy doesn't conform to a preconceived tinkling dream we were carrying around.

If Italians run into a time warp when they hit the old country, Eastern Italians from the older settlements in New York, New Jersey, Connecticut, Rhode Island, and Massachusetts have just as crazy a time when they leave the Eastern Seaboard and venture west.

The truth of the matter is that there aren't any real Italians beyond the Eastern Seaboard, and I know that a lot of people who claim they are Italians in places like

Wyoming and Montana are going to write to me saying there really are Italians. I don't think so. They may *think* they're Italians just because their names end in vowels, but that's about it. The only thing that makes us truly national is the Mafia. It has branches throughout the country in the top forty markets (as they say in the media business). But those people in Saint Louis who happen to have a vowel at the end of their names are a different breed from the Italian Italians I know.

Saint Louis is supposed to have a strongly defined Italian population. They've got a ghetto there called "The Hill" and there's always a lot of talk about how Italian Saint Louis is. Not so. I've got a friend named Bob who has a vowel at the end of his name and lives in Saint Louis. He *thinks* he's Italian, but he really isn't. He's a heavyset guy, and he's always talking about pizza and Mama Mia kind of things. And then I'll ask him how he happened to get into the marketing business. And he'll say, "Well, when I graduated from the University of Missouri I . . ." Then I know he's not Italian. I realize that he probably had to take a course at the University of Missouri called "Son of Immigrants 201" where they taught him how to speak halting second-generation Italian.

Bob will say to me, "Come on, Jerry, let's go to this fantastic Italian restaurant we've got." Off we go and it's not Italian food. It's nice food and all that, but it's not Italian.

Most Italian restaurants out of town are called either Anthony's or Tony's. When it's Anthony's they serve fancier food and have higher prices. Tony's tends to be more of a quick-turnover place. I've found very few Italian restaurants in New York called Anthony's. We've got La Casa

This, or Chateau That, or the Villa Herbie, but we don't have Anthony's. Yes, on Irving Place there's a terrific restaurant called *Sal* Anthony's and it's across the street from another fantastic restaurant called Paul *and* Jimmy's, but please notice, no plain Anthony's or Tony's.

Most Italian restaurants in most American cities turn out to be the place where they put canned tomato sauce on bread and call it pizza, or maybe if they're cute they put the sauce on English muffin halves.

The tendency out of town is to believe that the Italian restaurant really can't make it on its own. For example, the flashy Italian restaurant in Los Angeles is called La Scala. It's all right as restaurants go — Mimi Sheraton in the *Times* probably would give it one star and a push — but the owners of La Scala felt they needed something to put their place over so they got George Raft to front the place. He's the greeter — not the maître d'hôtel — but a glad hand when you get through the front door.

Talk about your folks with rhythm and other stereotypes. The owners of the restaurant figured George Raft played the part of a gangster in one hundred movies and since in the public's eye gangster is Italian, let's put George out in front. You don't see George Raft in front of a Jewish restaurant on Fairfax Avenue. And that terrific Chinese restaurant, Mr. Chow's, didn't need him either. Only the Italians would have the, ah, *chutzpah* to do a thing like that. George doesn't play the Mexican restaurants down on Alvaro Street — he's strictly Italian.

Although the people in Los Angeles do have one restaurant which passes itself off as Italian, try and find a grocery store to buy some Italian provisions. I once tried and found it practically impossible. My wife and I had rented a house out in Los Angeles one spring, and when Easter rolled around we decided on a typical Italian home-cooked meal. Now we weren't in the middle of Montana looking for fresh ricotta, or in some tiny spot in Texas, we were in one of the most heavily populated areas in the United States with a metropolitan population of twenty million people in an area of more than five hundred square miles.

Nothing in the way of a grocery store. And we needed real sausages, real pasta, lasagna, fresh ricotta and mozzarella, and real Italian tomato sauce, not the junk you get in jars. The first twenty people we asked turned out to be Mexicans, not Italians, and we were thrown by their skin. They looked at Barbara and me as if we were crazy. They only knew about fresh tortillas.

In desperation, we started haunting the all-night supermarkets, which are all over L.A. But they barely carried any Italian foods, much less the real article. Our problem, when we got through asking Mexicans and finally reached what were called genuine L.A. Italians, was they weren't Italians at all. I spoke to about five guys, each one standing there with maybe one hundred pounds of gold chains hanging around his neck. He may have been an Italian at one time, but I couldn't tell it now. They all looked like fucking Inca princes, or at the very least Montezuma. They all had their standard five gold bracelets, four gold rings, eighteen gold chains, one gold coke spoon, and a shirt cut down to the belly. I might just as well have been speaking Arabic when I asked these guys where I could find some fresh ricotta that didn't taste like farmer's cheese.

We were lucky, though. I ran into a guy from Chicago would you believe named Sid Cohen who said he thought there was a real grocery store down on Vermont Avenue.

Sure enough, in this bum location was a small, old, tired Italian guy barely making ends meet selling the real thing. We stocked up and finally got to cook our Italian meal, the first true home-cooked meal in the State of California.

Once the Italians got out of New York City, their integration was complete. The guy from New York named Di Nobile who used to live between Russo and Califano now lives between Smith and Jones. Di Nobile may be living in the San Fernando Valley, but he sure as hell isn't going to find any local Italian grocery out there. Or anywhere else, as I found out. In fact, the citizens of a place like Orange County still think that the only reason they see an occasional Italian around is because he's still building the railroad.

If the New York Italian loses his identity the moment he leaves the Holland Tunnel, check the Los Angeles Mexican, who is awfully similar to the New York Italian. In Los Angeles, the Mexicans look and sound just the way we Italians look and sound in New York. They're suspicious, they couldn't care less about the English language, they live in their own ghetto, and the older inhabitants rarely try to get out of the confining life-style. Like the Italians in New York with the New York City cops, the Mexicans don't talk and won't trust the L.A. police. The Mexicans gamble among themselves, have the same poor medical, dental, and legal facilities available to them as the New York Italians have, and are similar to Italians I know in Brooklyn in dozens of ways.

However, the moment Mexicans (especially younger, second-generation Mexicans) can escape the ghetto and leave Los Angeles, they are different people. They blend into society and seem to be accepted more readily than they would be in their hometown of Los Angeles, where in many quarters they're still cursed at. The Mexicans I meet on the streets of New York are light-years apart from L.A. Mexicans. In fact, they're very busy trying to make sure nobody thinks they're Puerto Rican.

I'm staggered when I hear that there are any — much less a large community of — Italians in a place like Saint Louis. I figure maybe the first Italian heard Saint Louis and thought "saint" — what the hell, it sounds Italian — and off he went. I also think that the Italians, the Greeks, the Poles, the Germans, and all of the other groups were brave as hell to get beyond New York City. It's not an accident that everything that happened in the Italian experience took place within a three- or four-block radius of Mulberry Street. Then one person decided to chance it and try Brooklyn, and the others followed.

But the Italians who made it to Saint Louis and San Francisco did not even stop in New York, because if they had they would have rooted here and never have gone West. They arrived; they had the name of an intrepid cousin out in San Francisco, and off they went. It took a certain amount of courage to pick up and leave Naples for the New World, but the Italian who left Mulberry Street for Wyoming (and I doubt that there is one Italian in that state) was a truly brave son-of-a-bitch.

A lot of Italians hit Ellis Island and followed the ocean, literally, ending up in places like Providence and Boston. In most cases of immigration to the Eastern Seaboard, the Italians went North rather than South. We ended up in terrific spots like Buffalo, Hartford, and Utica, rather than going down to Baltimore, Washington, Norfolk. How would you like to be an Italian in Virginia? Better yet, how'd you like to be an Italian in Arkansas? Check out the number of Italians in Mississippi.

There are no Italians in Seattle so far as I can figure. When I go to Seattle on business the town might as well run a headline in the local paper, saying, "Italian Visits Town." Somehow, there were a few Italians in Kansas City during the old Harry Truman Machine days and they were involved in local politics. And then someone in town hired a couple of out-of-town Italian killers and the only two local Italians were bumped off, thereby ending the line.

In Saint Louis, people talk about "The Hill," as if it were some hotshot big Italian community. Joe Garagiola talks about it during his sports programs, and whenever Yogi Berra is interviewed and is asked about Saint Louis, he talks nostalgically about "The Hill." Well, it might be a ghetto, but somehow it doesn't sound extraordinarily Italian. Yes, I think it probably was a tough neighborhood — but the world is full of tough neighborhoods. I listen to Joe Garagiola on the air and I keep coming away with the feeling that he's not *quite* Italian. I don't believe that "The Hill" had that wall built around it that we had — the anger, the hostility, the suspicion. Garagiola is simply too fucking cheerful to have come out of the real horrendous Italian ghetto.

There *seems* to be a similarity in the Italian neighborhoods along the Eastern Seaboard. I have been through streets in Boston's North End that are absolutely the same as Prince Street, Hester Street, Mulberry Street, in New York. I have seen two-family houses in Buffalo that are identical to those in Queens. And I am quite sure that life is the same. In New York the daughter lives with the family until she's married. She gets married and then she and her husband move downstairs from her parents. When you ask the mother where her daughter is living, she'll look at you with surprise and say, "Why, she's living downstairs from me. What'd you think?" After eleven months and a few hours, the young couple have the first kid. Then they buy *their* two-family house out on Long Island and her parents come along and live downstairs. That's their life. The only change, perhaps, is that after being married for about twenty-five years, the young couple take a charter trip to Italy and naturally the trip turns out to be a bummer, with the woman hiding her jewelry in the bottom of her pocketbook.

This is radically different from my friend in Saint Louis who went to college, played football, and now has a good job in a corporation. New York simply didn't produce any Italian football players. Football in the 1940s and 1950s was linked in many ways to education, and we Italians were definitely not linked to education in many ways.

The Italians in the rest of the country are one hell of a lot better off than their New York counterparts. In Brooklyn, they're still sitting around blaming the Jews for everything. Out there, the Italians are just as mobile as the rest of the population. *They're* normal. *We're* not.

One of the things I hope is changing is the Italian image. There was a time that whenever you looked at a movie coming out of Hollywood it appeared we were a nation of barbers. And if not barbers, at the very least shoemakers. The blacks were shufflin', smilin', and singin' spirituals. We were cutting hair and fixing shoes. I still have a picture in my mind that if there are two Italians living in Muncie,

Indiana, one of them is a barber and the other is a shoemaker. Now I know that's wrong. (The third Italian is a tile contractor.)

In some ways it's very tough for us to leave, despite our efforts. Once a year they throw a festival in New York City called the Festival of San Gennaro. During the festival about half a million people jam a four-block area over a period of five or six days to eat sausages and get sick. But when I look at the people at San Gennaro, I find that they're mostly from New Jersey and Long Island, back in town to get a fix of ethnic background. Those folks in their double-knits with their mouths stuffed just can't walk away from their past that easily.

Although we are outgrowing the image of the shoemaker and the barber, the Italian today is now trying to cope with the latest image, thanks to Mario Puzo. His novel, *The Godfather*, did more for us than any work of art since *The Untouchables*. Puzo made us out to be mysterious, sinister, exciting, vindictive, *sexy*. He took the Italians as a group and glamorized us, which can't have been easy. Before Puzo, most of the people in the country had us one step above gypsies. People didn't know who told fortunes and who didn't. In fact, a lot of folks got us confused because the adjectives were the same: we (as well as the gypsies) are brooding, lustful, haunting, hungry, exciting, and on and on. There are a lot of Italian guys out there getting laid when they normally wouldn't be just because Puzo made us out to be swashbucklers who belonged in one of those Rosemary Rogers paperback romances. Even straight Italians living in Italian retirement villages called Phoenix and Tucson benefited from Puzo's treatment of us.

Sadly, *The Godfather* was not quite accurate. Much

more to the point is Henry Winkler's portrayal of The Fonz on television. Although it isn't spelled out, The Fonz is truly Italian — the real thing — right down to his deses, dems, and doses. His New York accent is close to an Italian accent. His carrying on, cutting up, fooling around, is out of the neighborhood. I could take The Fonz and put him on Avenue U and nobody would bat an eyelash. His portrayal is accurate even down to his friends. I know that his buddies are all going to amount to something and get out of there, but I also know that The Fonz, like so many Italians, is not going to leave. The rest of the world will graduate into society but not The Fonz. He'll be hanging around on the corner, looking for action, hustling and carping, wondering why the world passed him by.